DESSERT RECIPES

for

Chocolate LOVERS!

DESSERT RECIPES

for

Chocolate
LOVERS!

THE MOST DECADENT RECIPES FOR
CAKES, PIES, BROWNIES, COOKIES,
FUDGE, ICE-CREAM & MORE!

LESLIE TAYLOR

Published by:
SweetiePieBooks.com
Publisher@sweetiebooks.com

ISBN: 978-0615848259

Copyright 2013 by Lisa Joy Taylor and SweetiePieBooks.com. All rights reserved. Unless otherwise noted, no part of this book may be reproduced, stored in a retrieval system, transmitted in any form or by any means, electronic, mechanical photocopying, recoding or transmitted in any form without express written permission from the author, except for brief quotations or critical reviews.

TABLE OF CONTENTS

INTRODUCTION 7

FOR THE LOVE OF CHOCOLATE 11

CAKES 19

PIES 45

CHOCOLATE DECADENCE – OVER
THE TOP DESSERTS 67

BROWNIES/BARS 87

ICE CREAM, GELATO, AND SORBET 107

MOUSSE 137

PUDDING 177

COOKIES 189

TARTS 209

FUDGE 219

TRUFFLES 229

ABOUT THE AUTHOR 235

DESSERT RECIPES FOR CHOCOLATE LOVERS!

INTRODUCTION

Chocolate... we love it soooooo much. For many of us it is a passion!

And if you are crazy about chocolate – then you are going to love this book!

In this chocolate dessert recipe book, Chef Leslie Taylor shares over 87 of his favorite chocolate dessert recipes, including chocolate cakes, pies, cookies, brownies, bars, fudge, a variety of ice creams and mousses, tarts and a very special section called Chocolate Decadence, which features tantalizing, over the top chocolate recipes!

Here are a few of the mouthwatering dessert ideas you'll discover in this book:

Nutella Stuffed Brown Butter and Sea Salt Chocolate Chip Cookies

Chocolate Espresso Cupcakes w/Kahlua Cream Cheese Frosting

Double Chocolate Cheesecake

Chocolate Three-Milk Cake

Red Wine Chocolate Cake with Whipped Mascarpone

Chocolate French Silk Pie

Chocolate Caramel Macadamia Tart

Dark Chocolate Cherry Brownies w/ Ganache and Sea Salt

Sicilian Chocolate Gelato with Bourbon and Dark Chocolate Chips

And in the chapter, *For the Love of Chocolate* you'll discover a few tasty morsels of information that every chocolate lover wants to know including:

- Why we love chocolate so much
- The health benefits of eating chocolate
- The history of chocolate
- How it is made
- The difference among milk, dark, and white chocolates
- And more!

Whether you enjoy the occasional sweet or you are a confirmed chocoholic this chocolate dessert recipe collection is sure to become one of your favorite dessert recipe collections.

FOR THE LOVE OF CHOCOLATE…

Whether you are 8 or 80, we all love chocolate! Not only does chocolate taste amazing, but it has been scientifically proven to increase our mood and benefit our health! This is very reassuring for those of us who see eating chocolate as an important part of life. So, why do we love chocolate so much?

A study out of the University of Michigan is busy uncracking this very mystery. Chocolate, researchers say, is literally like a drug making us feel better with every bite. In addition to the amazing taste, chocolate can lift our spirits since it contains a number of chemicals that do just that including:

Theobromine: a mild stimulant that promotes a positive mental attitude and increases alertness.

Anandamine: effects on the brain are very similar to (though much milder and more legal) marijuana.

Phenylethylamine: a neurotransmitter which stimulates the brain's pleasure centers.

Trytophan: triggers serotonin, a feel good chemical which produces feelings of elation.

What's more, this intriguing and surprisingly healthy delicacy is also incredibly versatile taking on a huge variety of shapes and forms, including candy bars, cakes, pies, cookies, puddings, tortes, chocolate dipped fruit, ice cream, beverages, such as hot chocolate and smoothies, as well as *in* or *on* whatever the imagination can come up with!

THE HISTORY OF CHOCOLATE

Dating back almost 4,000 years ago, Aztec kings were some of the first known to adore chocolate, offering the beans to the gods and drinking it religiously at ceremonies. The Mayan society saw cacao as a gift from God and worshipped it accordingly. In fact, the Mayan translation for cacao is "good food."

Recently, architects from the University of Pennsylvania discovered cacao residue on pottery from Honduras that dates back to 1400 BCE. They believe the cacao beans were crushed up and then used in an alcoholic drink of some kind.

It wasn't until the 1500's that cocoa was introduced to Europe when Cortez presented King Charles V, the King of Spain, with the beans. It was in Spain that sweeteners and other flavors were added to chocolate and it soon became a favored drink of the aristocracy.

Spain kept this tantalizing treat a secret from the rest of Europe for the next 100 years at which time it started to spread to neighboring countries, including England, where in London fashionable "chocolate houses" started popping up. The British were also the first to turn chocolate in a solid confection in 1830 by J. S. Fry & Sons.

And it was in 1755 that the United States was introduced to chocolate and the production of this confection grew at a faster pace than anywhere else in the world at this time.

During World War II the U.S. government made chocolate bars standard issue to soldiers, which they could use for quick energy and strength; a practice that continues today.

HOW CHOCOLATE IS MADE

Making chocolate is a multi-step process. Chocolate starts with the harvesting of cacao pods from cocoa trees. The pods are then split open and the bean inside, along with the pulp, is scraped and left to ferment for a few days. After fermentation, the beans are left to dry in direct sunlight.

The cacao beans are put into a large roasting machine where they come out warm, shaded a rich brown and ready to be cracked apart. Inside each cacao bean are nibs that contain the cocoa solids and cocoa butter, the part of the chocolate bean that we actually eat. All of these little nibs are sorted together and heated up so that they melt into what is called chocolate liqueur (sans any actual alcohol.) This is the foundation for all chocolate products.

The liqueur is then pressed, which removes the cocoa butter. This leaves a powdery disc called "cocoa press cake" and when pulverized becomes cocoa powder. From here, every chocolate company has a different way of conducting business. For milk chocolate, milk and sugar are added. For higher quality chocolates the cocoa butter is added back in to the chocolate liqueur, along with ingredients such as sugar, vanilla, and milk. White chocolate undergoes a similar process, except it does not contain chocolate liqueur or cocoa powder.

The last major step is called "conching," which massages the chocolate mixture anywhere from a few hours to few days. The conching makes the chocolate smooth and mellows any remaining acidic tones. After conching, the chocolate is tempered in large machines that cool the chocolate to precise temperatures in order to produce shiny, smooth bars. At this point, the chocolate is poured into molds then wrapped and shipped to chocolate lovers around the world.

It is also important to note that like wine, where a bean originates has everything to do with how it will taste. Beans from different locations have distinct differences. The majority (approximately two thirds) of the world's chocolate originates from Western Africa. Other cacao beans are farmed in places such as Brazil, Trinidad, Mexico, or Venezuela.

THE IMPORTANCE OF CACAO

The darker a chocolate bar is, the more cacao percentage it boasts. In turn, the higher percentage of cacao a chocolate bar contains, the higher quality chocolate it is. Think of it like this, if a chocolate bar is 50% cacao that means the other 50% are additives—which could include sugar, corn syrup, or a number of other equally unhealthy options.

Extremely dark, pure, and bitter chocolate can be anywhere from 85% to 99% cacao—of course this is the best option health-wise, but its intense taste makes it more popular for baking than eating. Anything that ranges from 35% to 84% in cacao is lumped into the "bittersweet" category—while 80% is still going to be quite bitter, 30% is rather sweet, so this is a very broad category. Lastly, chocolate that is 15% to 34% cacao is considered "semi-sweet;" think of the chocolate used in a Reese's Peanut Butter Cup for reference. Decide which cacao percent registers most favorably with your taste buds and remember that the more dark chocolate you eat, the more you will grow to love it.

EATING CHOCOLATE FOR BETTER HEALTH

Just hearing about how chocolate is made is enough to make anyone's mouth start to water, but before you panic about that new diet you're supposed to be on, keep in mind that chocolate is not your real enemy. Instead, it's the high content of sugar and milk products present in some of the more popular candy bars that can wreak havoc on your health. While in moderation, these candy bars won't kill you, but eating dark chocolate (which lacks the overload of additives) is a much healthier option.

BENEFITS OF DARK CHOCOLATE

Dark chocolate is not only better for you than milk chocolate, it's actually loaded with incentives. While you can count on your heartbeat improving, thanks to dark chocolate, you can also spare yourself some of the damage done by free radicals. Free radicals create permanent harm from smoking, fried foods, and a lot of normal everyday stuff, but research has found that chocolate miraculously erases some free radical damage. Dark chocolate is beneficial, largely due to the antioxidants it provides us, increasing the overall health of our blood and our bodies.

WHAT ABOUT WHITE CHOCOLATE?

White chocolate is commonly put into question; not only does it look, taste, and melt differently than its darker brother, its makeup is quite different as well. White chocolate is lacking many of the antioxidants found in regular cacao due to the stripping process it undergoes at the factory. While dark and milk chocolate undergo the same stripping process, the cocoa solids are replaced into chocolate at a later time while they remain forever vacant in white chocolate. Interestingly, there are laws permitting any white chocolate from being over 55% sugar in America.

LONG LIVE CHOCOLATE

As I write this I can't help but think, what will chocolatiers come up with next? What other ways will there be to enjoy this delicacy and what more can we do with cacao beans? The options are unlimited. Just think, a couple-hundred years ago we didn't even know you could serve chocolate as a solid and now you can buy it in 50 different flavors at every gas station, corner store and supermarket around the world. Amen!

DESSERT RECIPES FOR CHOCOLATE LOVERS!

CAKES

DOUBLE CHOCOLATE CHEESECAKE

INGREDIENTS

24 chocolate sandwich cookies, crushed {about 2 cups}

¼ cup butter or margarine, melted

4 ounce. pkg. cream cheese, softened

1 cup sugar

2 tablespoons flour

1 teaspoon vanilla

1 pkg. (8 squares) Baker's semi-sweet chocolate, melted and cooled {any other brand of baking chocolate would also work, this just seems to be the most popular brand}

4 eggs

COOKING INSTRUCTIONS

1. Preheat the oven to 325 degrees F. In a bowl, mix together the cookie crumbs and butter. Press the mixture into the bottom of a 9 x 13 pan that is lined with foil. Bake for 10 minutes.

2. Use an electric hand mixer to beat the cream cheese, sugar, flour and vanilla. Add the chocolate and mix well. While mixing the filling on low, add in the eggs, one at a time, just until blended. Pour the mixture over the crust.

3. Bake for about 45 minutes until center is almost set. Remove from the oven and cool. Refrigerate for about 4 hours.

4. Using the foil, lift the cheesecake from pan. Best served with berries or whipping cream on top.

CHOCOLATE ESPRESSO CUPCAKE WITH KAHLUA CREAM CHEESE FROSTING

Yield: 30 cupcakes

INGREDIENTS

Cupcakes:

1 cup butter, softened to room temperature

1 ¾ cups sugar

2 eggs

2 teaspoons vanilla extract

1 cup buttermilk or 1 cup whole milk with 1 tablespoon lemon juice

½ cup strong coffee, cooled

2 cups flour

¾ cup cocoa powder

1 teaspoon baking soda

1 ½ teaspoons baking powder

½ teaspoon salt

Frosting:

8 ounce bar cream cheese, cold

½ cup butter (1 stick), softened to room temperature

1 teaspoon vanilla extract

4 tablespoons Kahlua coffee liqueur[1]

3 ½ cups powdered sugar, measure then sift

---

1. The amount of Kahlua can be adjusted for taste. For a stronger coffee flavor add more Kahula. If you want a non-alcoholic option, add 2 to 3 tablespoons of instant espresso powder and ½ cup granulated sugar to 1 cup of hot water and mix.

Topping:

½ to ¾ cup Kahlua coffee liqueur*

1 cup chocolate covered espresso beans

COOKING INSTRUCTIONS

1. Preheat oven to 350 degrees F. In three muffin pans place cupcake liners in each well. In a bowl put the butter and sugar and beat until it is light and fluffy. Slowly add each egg into the mixture one at a time. In a separate bowl, sift together the flour, cocoa powder, baking soda, baking powder and salt. Combine the buttermilk and coffee together. Mix the flour and buttermilk mixture by alternately adding the two. Pour the batter into the prepared pans with liners. Bake until a toothpick inserted in the middle of the cupcake comes out clean. The cupcakes should cool for at least 10 minutes. Poke holes in the top of each cupcake. Over each cupcake drizzle about ½ teaspoon of Kahlua.

2. Using an electric hand mixer on a low speed beat the cream cheese and butter until blended. Add in the vanilla and Kahlua. Next, mix in the powdered sugar one cup at a time. After adding the powdered sugar, increase the mixer to a higher speed. Whip up the frosting until it is light and fluffy. Add the frosting to a piping bag.

3. Lightly crush the chocolate covered espresso beans into smaller pieces in a freezer bag, using a rolling pin. Put the frosting on each cupcake. Drizzle some Kahlua on

top of the frosting. Then sprinkle the espresso bean pieces over the Kahlua and frosting.

CHOCOLATE CAKE WITH CHOCOLATE GANACHE

INGREDIENTS

Cake:

1 large egg

1 cup granulated sugar

6 ounces plain, vanilla, or chocolate yogurt (thicker Greek-style preferred, do not use diet, fat-free or light yogurt; sour cream may be substituted)

¼ cup canola or vegetable oil

1 ½ teaspoons vanilla extract

½ cup brewed coffee, room temperature or warm

½ cup unsweetened natural cocoa powder (Hershey's is the best)

1 cup all-purpose flour

1 teaspoon baking soda

½ teaspoon baking powder

½ teaspoon salt, optional

COOKING INSTRUCTIONS

1. Preheat the oven to 350 degrees F. Line a 9 x 9 inch square baking pan with aluminum foil. Spray the foil with cooking oil or grease. Flour a 10-inch round cake pan; set aside.

2. Thoroughly mix the egg, sugar, yogurt, oil and vanilla in a large bowl and whisk until smooth. Add in the coffee and cocoa powder. Whisk the mixture vigorously. The

batter should be smooth and have no lumps. Continue to vigorously whisk the mixture while adding the flour, baking soda, baking powder and salt until the batter has just combined. Note about coffee: I recommend that you use coffee instead of water. The coffee brings out the flavor of the cocoa powder rather than make the cake taste like coffee. To prevent cooking the eggs, use coffee that is not "piping hot." The batter will be pretty loose and runny. Add the batter into the prepared pan and bake it for approximately 25 minutes. The cake will be done when the top has set and a toothpick or cake tester comes out clean after being inserted.

3. The cake needs to cool completely in the pan for approximately 30 minutes in order to be able to add the ganache or frosting. The cake should also be cooled before slicing or serving. Store the bare cake at room temperature for up to five days in an air tight container. A frosted cake can be stored in the refrigerator in an airtight container.

INGREDIENTS

Chocolate Ganache (microwavable):

9 ounces semi-sweet chocolate (about 1 ½ cups semi-sweet chocolate chips)

¾ cup cream or half-and-half

1 teaspoon vanilla extract

COOKING INSTRUCTIONS

1. Place the chocolate in a medium microwave-safe bowl. Put the bowl in the microwave and heat on high for one minute in order to soften the chocolate. Remove the bowl from the microwave and set it aside. Heat the cream (I use half-and-half) in a small microwave-safe bowl or measuring cup on high power until the liquid just begins to bubble. It should take about 60 to 75 seconds.

2. Pour the hot cream over chocolate. Allow to stand for about 1 minute. Next, whisk the cream and the chocolate vigorously until the chocolate has melted and mixture is smooth and velvety.

3. Stir in the vanilla and continue to combine. You can use optional flavorings to vanilla, if you like. Allow the ganache to cool for approximately ten minutes. The ganache will thicken somewhat.

4. Pour the ganache over the cake after whisking briefly. Spread the ganache over the top of the cake using a spatula or an offset knife.

5. Allow the cake to set for at least ½ hour at room temperature before slicing or serving. You may also serve the cake sooner by cooling it in the refrigerator or freezer briefly.

DOUBLE CHOCOLATE BLACK FOREST CAKE

INGREDIENTS

Chocolate Cake:

2 cups sugar

2 cups all-purpose flour

¾ cup cocoa

2 teaspoons baking powder

1 teaspoon baking soda

½ teaspoon salt

2 eggs

1 cup soured milk (just add a tablespoon of lemon juice or plain vinegar to a cup of milk)

1 cup black coffee

½ cup vegetable oil

1 teaspoon vanilla extract

COOKING INSTRUCTIONS

1. In a large mixing bowl mix all the ingredients using an electric mixer for two minutes.

2. Prepare two 9 inch cake pans by greasing and flouring. You may also dust the pans with cocoa instead. Pour the batter into the pans.

3. Bake the cake at 350 degrees F. Leave in the oven for 30 to 35 minutes or until a toothpick that is inserted in the center of the cake comes out clean.

4. Remove the cake from the oven to cool completely on a wire rack. Once cooled, split the two layers into four with a sharp serrated bread knife.

INGREDIENTS

Whipped Chocolate Ganache:

To make the filling/frosting use a double boiler to melt together the following:

3 cups dark chocolate chips

½ cup whipping cream

COOKING INSTRUCTIONS

1. Stir the mixture continually with the double boiler at a gentle simmer until melted and smooth. Do not overheat. Heat until the mix reaches the melting point and is lukewarm to the touch.

2. Move the mixture into a large mixing bowl.

3. Whip to firm peaks two cups whipping cream.

4. Fold the whipped cream into the chocolate mixture in four portions. Fold the mixture gently after each addition until the cream is completely combined with the chocolate.

5. For 30 minutes or more, chill the frosting in the freezer, if it is too soft to work with. Be sure to fold the frosting with a rubber spatula every 10 minutes. This way it will cool evenly.

INGREDIENTS

Vanilla Whipped Cream:

2 cups whipping cream

4 rounded tablespoons icing sugar (powdered sugar)

2 teaspoons vanilla extract

Whip together to firm peaks.

1 pound ripe fresh cherries, pitted and chopped

Chocolate for garnish.

COOKING INSTRUCTIONS

1. To construct the cake, use a sharpened serrated knife to cut the two cakes into four. Place the first piece of cake on a cake plate and cover it with the whipped cream, followed by the next piece of cake. Add a thin layer of the ganache on this layer followed by a layer of pitted cherries. Top the cherries with a layer of the ganache that will totally cover the cherries.

2. On top of the last layer of cherries, put the next cake layer along with more whipped cream, followed by the final cake layer. Use the ganache to ice the entire outside of the cake. Use the rest of the whipped cream to create a border. Frost the entire outside of the cake with the remaining whipped ganache frosting and place another layer of pitted cherries on top of the cake. Garnish with borders of vanilla whipped cream and with chopped chocolate on the sides.

CHOCOLATE RASPBERRY BAVARIAN TORTE

INGREDIENTS

Chocolate Genoise:

3 large eggs plus 3 large egg yolks, at room temperature

¾ cup granulated sugar

⅛ teaspoon salt

⅓ cup cake flour

⅓ cup cornstarch

¼ cup unsweetened alkalized cocoa powder

Raspberry Syrup:

¼ cup sugar

⅓ cup water

¼ cup raspberry liqueur

Over medium heat, combine the sugar and water in a saucepan until boiled. Remove from heat and allow to cool. Stir in liqueur.

COOKING INSTRUCTIONS

1. Preheat the oven to 350 degrees F. Prepare an 8-inch round baking pan by greasing the pan and lining it with parchment paper.

2. Using an electric hand mixer at high speed, beat together whole eggs, egg yolks, sugar and salt in a heat-proof bowl (preferably stainless). Put the bowl over simmering water in a pan. Continue beating with an electric hand mixer until the contents are warm. Take the bowl

from the pan of water. For approximately 5 to 7 minutes beat the mixture until the volume has increased and the batter is thick enough to leave a trail back into the bowl from the beaters.

3. Using a sifter, mix together the cake flour, cornstarch and cocoa. Next, sift the dry ingredients over the egg mixture. Use a spatula to gently fold the ingredients. Pour the batter in the prepared pan.

4. Bake until the cake springs back when touched with a finger, approximately 30 minutes. Remove from the oven and cool on a wire rack in the pan for ten minutes. Use a knife to loosen the edge of the cake. Flip the cake onto a rack. Remove the baking paper carefully. Place another rack over the top of the cake and flip again. Allow the cake to cool completely.

INGREDIENTS

Raspberry Bavarian:
2 bags (12 ounces each) frozen unsweetened raspberries
¾ cup sugar
⅓ cup raspberry liqueur
2 envelopes unflavored gelatin powder (½ ounce.)
2 cups heavy cream

COOKING INSTRUCTIONS

1. Allow the frozen raspberries to thaw in the bags. Combine the entire contents of the thawed raspberries, including all the juice and the sugar, in a saucepan. Heat the contents to a boil and simmer for 10 minutes. Using a fine-mesh sieve, strain the mixture into a bowl. This should yield approximately 2 cups of raspberry juice and pulp. Cool the raspberry mixture to room temperature.

2. In a heatproof cup, mix the liqueur and gelatin. Let stand for 5 minutes. Put the cup into the microwave and heat until the gelatin becomes liquid. This should take approximately 10 seconds. This can also be done in a saucepan over the stove, if you prefer.

3. Whisk the liqueur and gelatin into raspberry purée.

4. Using an electric mixer on high speed, beat the heavy cream in a bowl until stiff peaks form. Fold the completed raspberry mixture into the whipped cream.

ASSEMBLY:

1 cup chocolate-hazelnut spread, heated until loosened considerably

1 ½ cups whipped cream

Dark chocolate curls or shavings

26 to 28 fresh raspberries (about 1 ½ pints)

1. Use a serrated knife to level the cake. Cut the genoise horizontally into two equal layers. Place one half of the cake in the centered in the bottom of a 9-inch springform pan. Be sure the cut side is up. Using a pastry brush, apply half of the raspberry syrup. On top of the syrup, use a spatula to lay out ½ cup of the chocolate-hazelnut spread evenly.

2. On top and around the sides of the cake pour ½ of the raspberry Bavarian cream. Drop the pan gently on the counter top a couple of times to make sure the cream settles into the empty circle around the genoise. Top with the other half of the cake. Spread the rest of the chocolate-hazelnut spread over the genoise. Use what is left of the Bavarian cream to top the cake. Drop the pan on the counter top gently as before. The cream should completely fill the 9-inch pan with a little left over. Use a large off-set spatula to even out the top. Cover the pan and refrigerate for at least 2 hours until the mixture sets.

3. Run a small knife between dessert and pan. Take out the springform collar. Spread 1 cup whipped cream on side of dessert. Pipe a decorative border using a small star decorator tip (if desired) with the rest of the whipped cream. On the sides of the cake press the chocolate curls or shavings. Sprinkle center with chocolate curls, as well.

DARK CHOCOLATE FROSTED YELLOW CAKE WITH RASPBERRY PRESERVES

INGREDIENTS

Cake:

1 box yellow cake mix

1 scant cup water (a little less than a cup, but more than ¾)

⅓ cup butter, melted

3 eggs

Raspberry Filling:

1 cup frozen raspberries, thawed and drained

⅔ cup raspberry preserves

Dark Chocolate Frosting:

½ cup plus 1 tablespoon unsweetened cocoa powder

½ cup plus 1 tablespoon boiling water

2 ¼ cups (4 ½ sticks) unsalted butter, room temperature

2 cups powdered sugar, sifted

¼ teaspoon salt

1 ½ pounds semisweet chocolate, melted and cooled

12 ounces mini chocolate chips for decorating

COOKING INSTRUCTIONS

1. Preheat the oven to 350 degrees F. Prepare two 9 inch round cake pans by greasing the pan and sprinkling with flour. With an electric mixer combine the cake mix, water, butter and eggs in a large mixing bowl for 1 minute. Be sure to scrape the sides of the bowl and then mix on high for one minute. Pour the batter evenly into the two pans you prepared.

2. Bake the cakes until a toothpick inserted in the cakes comes out clean. This should take about 25 to 30 minutes. Cool in the pan for ten minutes before removing. Cool the cakes completely.

3. Mix the raspberries and preserves in a small bowl.

4. Put one of the cakes face down on a cardboard with two pieces of parchment paper between the cake and the cardboard. Spread the cake with the raspberry mixture. Be sure to leave a 1-inch border. Add the second cake with the bottom side up over the raspberries.

5. Add the cocoa to the boiling water. Stir until the cocoa has dissolved. Beat the butter, powdered sugar and salt until whiteish in color and fluffy using an electric mixer on medium-high. Reduce the mixer to low speed. Add in the melted and cooled chocolate. Beat until the mixture is combined, making sure that you scrape down the sides of the bowl as needed. Finally, beat in the cocoa mixture.

6. Frost the cake. Remove the parchment paper from underneath the cake. Top the cake with the mini-chocolate chips.

BOCA NEGRA CHOCOLATE CAKE

INGREDIENTS

Optional White Chocolate Cream:

12 ounces. white chocolate, chopped

1 cup heavy cream

¼ cup bourbon

Cake:

12 ounces bittersweet or semi-sweet chocolate, chopped

1 and ⅓ cup sugar

½ cup bourbon

8 ounces (2 sticks) butter, room temperature and cut into 10 pieces

5 large eggs, room temperature

1.5 tablespoons all-purpose flour

COOKING INSTRUCTIONS

Make the optional cream the day before:*

1. In a food processor or blender place the chopped chocolate.

2. Heat the cream until it just begins to boil in a saucepan.

3. Add the hot cream over the chocolate. Mix until smooth in the blender or food processor.

4. Stir in the bourbon.

5. Store in the refrigerator in an airtight container.

Cake:

1. Preheat the oven to 350 degrees F.

2. Prepare a 9-inch cake pan for baking. Cut out a circle of parchment paper to fit into the bottom of the pan. Next, butter the pan without the parchment circle in the bottom. Place the parchment circle in pan. Butter the top of the paper well.

3. Find an oven-safe roasting pan/dish that will fit a 9-inch cake pan. Add boiling water to the pan. Set aside to use as a water bath for once the cake is baked.

4. In a food processor or blender place the chopped chocolate.

5. Bring the sugar and bourbon to a full boil in a saucepan.

6. Add the sugar and bourbon mixture to the chocolate. Use the food processor blender to mix until smooth.

7. While the blender or food processor is running, add in the butter one piece at a time. Next, add in each egg,

one at a time. Finally, add the flour and blend/process for approximately 15 seconds or so.

8. Add the batter into the prepared cake pan. Set the cake pan in the water bath. Add the hot water to the bath until it comes up halfway on the sides of the pan.

9. Bake for 30 minutes. Once done, top of the cake should have a dry crust.

10. Remove the cake from the oven and then the water bath. Dry the pan with a towel. Cover the top of the cake with plastic wrap. Flip the cake onto a sheet pan or flat plate.

11. Take the pan off the cake. Carefully remove the parchment paper. Flip the cake once again onto a serving platter. Remove the plastic wrap and allow the cake cool.

12. The cake can be served either at room temperature or slightly warmer. The cake can be stored at room temperature for several days. Serve with the optional white chocolate cream or ice cream, crème anglaise or sweetened whipped cream.

Notes: This cream is not necessary. This cake tastes great on its own. Alternatively, you can add a bit of ice cream, crème anglaise (i.e. melted ice cream) or sweetened whipped cream.

CHOCOLATE CARAMEL DOUGHNUT HOLES

INGREDIENTS

2 ½ cups all-purpose flour, plus more for work surface

1 cup cocoa powder

2 teaspoons baking powder

½ teaspoon baking soda

1 ½ teaspoons coarse salt

1 cup sugar, plus more for coating

¾ cup low-fat buttermilk

4 tablespoons unsalted butter, melted

2 large eggs

28 to 30 store bought soft caramel squares, unwrapped

5 to 6 cups vegetable oil for frying

COOKING INSTRUCTIONS

1. Using a sifter, mix together the flour, cocoa powder, baking powder, baking soda and salt into a large bowl. Using a whisk, mix together the sugar, buttermilk, butter and eggs in another bowl until combined well. Stir the buttermilk mixture into the flour mixture. Mix just until a smooth dough is formed.

2. Flour a work surface. Place the dough on the work surface and pat it flat. Then lightly flour the dough. The dough should be rolled out to ⅓ inch thickness. Use a 2 ½ inch cookie cutter to cut the dough into rounds. Re-roll the dough and cut the scraps.

3. In the center of each of the rounds put a caramel. Form the dough around the caramel. Roll the round into a smooth ball.

4. Use a paper towel to line a baking sheet. Fill a wide and shallow bowl with 1 inch of sugar. Heat 4 inches of oil in a large, heavy pot. Insert a candy thermometer into the oil and cook until it reaches 350 degrees F. In four separate batches, deep fry the doughnuts for 5 minutes. Turn each doughnut once with a slotted spoon. Do not burn the oil. Adjust the heat as needed.

5. Put doughnuts on to the prepared sheet. Cool partially for at least four minutes. Coat the doughnuts in sugar. Serve immediately for best taste.

CHOCOLATE HAZELNUT CAKE

INGREDIENTS

1 ⅓ cups hazelnuts, toasted and skinned (by rolling them between towels)

2 tablespoons flour

1 cup sugar

1 stick butter, softened

5 large eggs, separated, plus 1 egg yolk

6 ounces dark chocolate - the best quality you can afford - melted and cooled

¼ teaspoon salt

Powdered sugar for dusting, if desired

COOKING INSTRUCTIONS

1. Preheat oven to 350 degrees F. Grease a 9-inch springform pan. (I use cooking spray.)

2. In a food processor, finely grind the hazelnuts, flour and ¼ cup of the sugar. Mix the butter and remaining sugar until fluffy using an electric mixer. Add all the yolks one at a time. Beat well after each yolk. Mix in hazelnut mixture and chocolate.

3. In a separate bowl, whip the egg whites and salt until stiff peaks form. In the chocolate batter, gently fold in ⅓ of the egg whites at a time. Be careful not to deflate the batter.

4. Bake the cake for 45 to 50 minutes until a toothpick inserted in center comes out clean. Remove the cake from the oven and cool completely on a wire rack. Dust the cake with powdered sugar before serving.

CHOCOLATE SOUFFLÉ

INGREDIENTS

Vanilla Pastry Cream Base:

2 cups milk

1 ½ ounces butter

2 vanilla beans (split and scraped)

1 ½ ounces corn starch

4 egg yolks

Chocolate Soufflé:

3 ½ egg whites

1 ½ ounces sugar

Pinch of salt

1 ½ ounces vanilla pastry cream base

3.75 ounces chocolate

Butter 4 ramekins and coat with sugar

COOKING INSTRUCTIONS

1. Preheat oven to 425 F.

2. Add half the milk, entire butter and 2 vanilla beans into a saucepan.

3. Heat over a medium flame.

4. Pour the other half of milk into a bowl and beat with cornstarch and egg yolks to make slurry.

5. Stir in the slurry to the milk as it starts scalding and mix together and boil.

6. Remove from heat and leave aside.

7. Double boil and melt chocolate.

8. Beat eggs until frothy using a stand mixer on medium speed then increase one more speed and continue beating until stiff.

9. Combine 1 ½ ounces pastry cream with melted chocolate for the base.

10. Stir in meringue in three portions with the chocolate mixture and mix well.

11. Flatten the mixture using a spatula into ramekins and wipe rim with your thumb and bake for 11 to 12 minutes.

DESSERT RECIPES FOR CHOCOLATE LOVERS!

PIES

CHOCOLATE FRENCH SILK PIE

INGREDIENTS

Crust:

1 ¼ cups all-purpose flour

1 tablespoon sugar

½ teaspoon salt

3 tablespoons vegetable shortening

5 tablespoons unsalted butter, cut into ¼-inch pieces and chilled

4 to 6 tablespoons ice water

Filling:

1 cup heavy cream, chilled

3 large eggs

¾ cup sugar

2 tablespoons water

8 ounces. bittersweet chocolate, melted and cooled

1 tablespoon vanilla extract

8 tablespoons unsalted butter, cut into ½-inch pieces and softened

COOKING INSTRUCTIONS

Crust:

1. Combine the flour, sugar and salt in a food processor for about 10 seconds. Dot shortening over the top of the mixture and process for approximately 10 seconds more until it resembles coarse cornmeal. Dot butter pieces over the top and pulse until it looks like coarse crumbs. It should take about ten pulses of the food processor. Move the mixture to a medium sized bowl. Sprinkle 4 tablespoons of the water over the top. Using a stiff rubber spatula, stir until the dough sticks together. If the dough does not come together, add the remaining water. Add in 1 tablespoon of water at a time until it does. Turn dough out onto a sheet of plastic wrap and flatten into a 4-inch disk. The disk should be wrapped in plastic wrap and refrigerated for at least 1 hour, but it can be stored up to two days until ready for use.

2. Soften the chilled dough lightly at room temperature. The dough should be rolled into a 12-inch circle on a lightly floured surface. Transfer the dough to a 9-inch pie plate. Trim and crimp the edges. Cover the pie plate loosely with plastic wrap. The pie plate should be refrigerated for at least 20 minutes or up to one day.

3. Put the oven rack in the middle position. Preheat the oven to 375 degrees F. Prepare the chilled crust by lining it with aluminum foil and placing pie weights inside the crust. Bake for 25 to 30 minutes until the crust is light and looks dry. Take out the weights and foil. Bake until the crust is golden brown. This should take approximately 10 minutes. Set the pie crust on a wire rack. Let the pie cool to room temperature.

Filling:

1. Whip the cream using an electric hand-held mixer for two to three minutes until stiff peaks form. Cover the bowl and chill in the refrigerator. .

2. Place a large heatproof bowl over a medium saucepan filled with ½ inch of barely simmering water. Combine eggs, sugar and water in the bowl. Beat the ingredients with an electric hand-held mixer on medium heat. Continue beating the mixture until it is thick and it reaches 160 degrees F. This should take about 7 to 10 minutes. Remove bowl from the stove. Continue to beat until the ingredients turn fluffy and have cooled to room temperature for approximately 8 minutes.

3. Add in the chocolate and vanilla until incorporated with a whisk. Add in the butter a few pieces at a time until mixed well. Gently fold in the whipped cream with a spatula until no streaks remain. Add the filling to the cooled pie crust. Let set for at least 3 hours in the refrigerator. The pie can set for up to 24 hours. Add

sweetened whipped cream and chocolate shavings, if you like, to the top of the pie.

S'MORE PIE

INGREDIENTS

Graham Cracker Crust:

2 cups graham cracker crumbs

8 tablespoons (1 stick) butter, melted

COOKING INSTRUCTIONS

1. Preheat oven to 325 degrees F.

2. Mix together the graham cracker crumbs and melted butter in a medium bowl. Make sure the crumbs are evenly coated. Form the mixture into a 9 inch pie plate. Bake until fragrant. This should take about 8 to 10 minutes. Keep the oven running.

Chocolate Filling:

¾ cup heavy cream

¾ cup milk

10 ounces semi-sweet chocolate, chopped

Pinch of salt

2 eggs, whisked

1 bag of large marshmallows

COOKING INSTRUCTIONS

1. Whisk together cream and milk in a medium saucepan and then warm the pan over medium-low heat. Stir in chocolate. Mix until it has melted and is smooth. Add whisked eggs slowly. Again mix until smooth.

2. In the baked pie crust, pour the chocolate filling. Bake the pie for 15 to 20 minutes. The chocolate filling should set and not move when pie is lightly shaken. Remove from the oven.

3. Place marshmallows cut in half with kitchen shears in concentric circles over the top of the pie. Do this until the entire pie is covered.

4. Set oven to broil and place pie under the broiler. Broil until the marshmallows are lightly toasted for 2 to 5 minutes. Be sure to watch the marshmallows carefully to prevent burning.

5. The pie should chill in the refrigerator for 2 to 3 hours in order to set.

6. Cut the cold pie into slices with a knife sprayed with non-stick cooking spray. It is important that the pie is chilled because it will not cut well when warm. The pie can be eaten cold; however, slightly warm the pie slices in a microwave for 7 to 10 seconds before serving for the best results. It is amazing! You can drizzle the pie with chocolate sauce, if desired.

CHOCOLATE CARAMEL MACADAMIA TART

INGREDIENTS

Pastry:

1 ⅛ cups all-purpose flour

⅛ cup sugar

2 tablespoons unsweetened Dutch-process cocoa powder

¼ teaspoon salt

6 tablespoons (3 ounces) cold unsalted butter, cut into small pieces

1 large egg yolk, lightly beaten

½ teaspoon pure vanilla extract

1 to 2 tablespoons cold heavy cream or ice water

COOKING INSTRUCTIONS

Crust:

1. Using a food processor, pulse the flour, sugar, cocoa and salt until mixed. Once you add the butter, pulse the ingredients for about 10 seconds until they look like coarse corn meal. Next add in the yolk and vanilla along with 1 tablespoon water/cream. Mix with the food processor no longer than 30 seconds until the mixture just begins to hold together.

2. Check to see if the dough is too dry. If it is, add in the remaining cream or water.

3. Form the dough into a disk. Wrap the disk in plastic wrap. It should be stored in the refrigerator until firm

for at least 1 hour. It can be stored for up to two days before use.

Chocolate Caramel Macadamia Tart:

½ cup macadamia nuts, halved

1 cup sugar

2 tablespoons light corn syrup

2 tablespoons water

1 cup heavy cream

4 tablespoons unsalted butter

½ teaspoon pure vanilla extract

Pinch of coarse salt, preferably sea salt

8 ounces dark (bittersweet) chocolate, finely chopped

1 quantity of pastry (Pate Sucree Chocolate)

COOKING INSTRUCTIONS

1. Preheat the oven to 375 degrees F. Using parchment paper, roll out the dough in a rectangle to about ⅛ inch thick. Move the dough to a baking sheet and chill in the refrigerator for about ten minutes. After ten minutes has passed remove the dough from the refrigerator. Line a 14 x 5 inch tart pan with the dough. The tart pan should have a removable bottom. Make sure to press the dough into the corners of the pan. Use a fork to prick all over the bottom of the tart . The tart pan should chill for at least 15 minutes.

2. While the tart pan is chilling, toast the nuts on a rimmed baking sheet. Put them on the sheet in a single

layer for about 10 minutes. The nuts should be golden and fragrant. Take the baking sheet out of the oven and set them aside. Leave the oven on.

3. Line the tart pan with parchment paper making sure to press the paper into the edges. Fill the tart with dried beans or pie weights. Bake the tart for 20 minutes on a baking sheet. After 20 minutes, take out the parchment paper and the weights. Bake for approximately five to seven minutes more. Put the tart on a wire rack to cool completely.

4. **To make the caramel:** Over a medium heat, bring the sugar, light corn syrup and water to boil in a small sauce pan. Be sure to apply water on the sides of the pan with a pastry brush. This will prevent crystals from forming on the pan. Over a low heat, swirl the pan evenly until the caramel is a rich amber color. After removing the pan from the heat, add ¼ cup of cream butter, vanilla and salt. Be careful as it will spatter. Stir the mixture until it is smooth. Cool the mixture for a couple of minutes then stir in the nuts.

5. **To make the ganache:** Put the chocolate in a glass or metal bowl. In a small sauce pan boil the rest of the cream. Immediately pour the cream over the chocolate. The ganache should cool for about 10 minutes until slightly thickened.

6. Coat the pastry shell evenly with the ganache. Chill the shell in the refrigerator for approximately 10 minutes.

7. Pour the caramel into the chilled shell.

8. Refrigerate the tart until you are ready to serve.

CHOCOLATE CHIP COOKIE PIE

INGREDIENTS

1 unbaked 9-inch pie crust, homemade or store-bought.

2 large eggs

½ cup flour

½ cup white granulated sugar

½ cup packed brown sugar

¾ cup real butter, softened (1 ½ sticks)

1 cup chocolate chips (semi-sweet or dark works best, you might find milk too sweet)

1 cup chopped pecans (you are welcome to make it without nuts)

Vanilla ice cream or sweetened whipped cream for serving - a must!

Optional: chocolate sauce (honestly, doesn't really need chocolate sauce, but it looks pretty!)

COOKING INSTRUCTIONS

1. Preheat oven to 325 degrees F.

2. Using a large mixing bowl, beat the eggs until foamy with a hand-held mixer on a high speed. Next add in the flour, granulated sugar and brown sugar and beat with the hand-held mixer. Now beat in the butter. Stir in morsels and nuts. Spoon into pie shell.

3. Put the pie shell in to the oven and bake for approximately 55 to 60 minutes. When the knife is put in the

pie halfway between the center and the edge and it comes out clean, the pie is done. You may serve the pie slightly warmed. Cool on wire rack to the desire temperature. Best with ice cream or whipped cream.

COOKIES 'N' CREAM BROWNIE PIE

INGREDIENTS

4 Hershey's Cookies 'n' Creme Chocolate Candy Bars

½ cup sugar

½ cup butter

2 eggs, lightly beaten

½ teaspoon vanilla

1 cup flour

½ teaspoon baking powder

Pinch of salt

7 ounces sweetened condensed milk

¾ cup mini semi-sweet chocolate chips

COOKING INSTRUCTIONS

1. Preheat oven to 350 degrees F.

2. Over a low heat in a large saucepan, melt candy bars, sugar and butter.

3. Using a whisk, add in the eggs and vanilla. Next, whisk in the flour, baking powder and salt. The mixture should be stirred until well incorporated and smooth.

4. Bake the mix in a greased 9- inch springform pan for 20 minutes.

5. Immediately after removing the brownies from the oven, pour 7 ounces sweetened condensed milk over top.

6. Let cool after layering with chocolate chips.

CHOCOLATE SWEET POTATO PIE

INGREDIENTS

Crust:

¾ cup coconut flour

½ teaspoon ground cinnamon

1 tablespoon honey

2 large eggs

½ cup butter, melted

COOKING INSTRUCTIONS

1. Beat in the eggs and honey into the cooled melted butter.

2. In a mixing bowl, sift the coconut flour and cinnamon. Add in the eggs and butter gradually until the mixture comes together.

3. Take the mixture and press it into the sides of a 9-inch pie dish. This pastry won't act "normal." This is okay, it will turn out fine.

4. Use a fork to prick the bottom of the pan. Put the pan in the refrigerator to chill while you make the filling.

Filling:

1 large sweet potato (should be big enough for 2 cups of mashed potato)

2.75 ounces dark chocolate (I used 59%, I would've gone higher, but that was all I had)

2 tablespoons cocoa powder

½ cup, plus 3 tablespoons heavy cream

⅓ cup honey

2 large eggs

½ cup butter

COOKING INSTRUCTIONS

1. Take the peeled sweet potato and dice it. Boil the potato pieces for 30 minutes until they are tender.

2. Put the chocolate, honey and butter in a double boiler and melt. Set the mixture aside to cool.

3. In a blender or food processor mix the potato and 3 tablespoons of cream. (Do not mash the potato. When I tried, it stayed lumpy even after a great deal of mashing.)

4. Add the eggs and cream into the cooled chocolate and whisk. Slowly whisk the mixture into the sweet potato until a somewhat runny batter is formed.

5. Pour batter into the pie dish. Bake the pie at 375 degrees F for 20 minutes. Remove from oven and allow to cool. Place the pie in the refrigerator for at least 1 hour before serving.

MINI VANILLA CUSTARD TARTS WITH CHOCOLATE CRUSTS AND RASPBERRIES

(Yields about 1 dozen mini pies)

INGREDIENTS

Crust:

1 ½ cups all-purpose flour

4 tablespoons unsweetened cocoa powder

¼ cup sugar

½ teaspoon vanilla extract

1 egg

½ cup unsalted butter (1 stick)

5 to 7 tablespoons ice cold water

Topping:

10 ounces jar raspberry jam

6 ounce container fresh raspberries

Filling:

½ cup sugar

¼ cup all-purpose flour

2 cups whole milk

1 egg yolk, beaten

1 ½ teaspoons vanilla extract

1 vanilla bean, scraped

COOKING INSTRUCTIONS

1. **To prepare the dough:** Add the flour, cocoa powder, and sugar in a bowl with a whisk until completely combined. In another bowl, use a whisk to mix the vanilla and egg. Set this bowl aside. Using a box grater, grate the cold butter into the dry ingredients. Pinch the ingredients and butter together until a coarse meal is formed. You may also cut the butter into the flour mixture to create the "meal." Combine the egg mixture with the flour mixture thoroughly. Make the dough soft by adding in 5 tablespoons of the cold water. If needed, add more cold water, 1 tablespoon at a time, until the dough just combines. Wrap the dough in plastic wrap and refrigerate for 1 to 2 hours.

2. **To make the custard filling:** Whisk the sugar and flour in a medium pot. Put the pot on the stove over a medium heat and add the 2 cups of milk. Stir continuously for 10 to 15 minutes until the mixture begins to thicken. Whisk in the egg yolk quickly. This will keep the eggs from cooking immediately. Remove the pot from the stove. Stir in vanilla extract and vanilla bean. Set the pot aside.

3. **To make the chocolate crusts:** After the dough has been cooled for 1 to 2 hours it can be rolled out on a lightly floured surface. Once done it should be ⅛-inch thick. Cut large circles for bottom crusts. You should be able to get at least 12 crusts out of the dough. With a pastry brush coat the wells of your pie maker with

oil. Place four of the dough rounds into the pie maker using the pie-pressing tool. Keep the dough from puffing up while baking by pricking the dough all over with a fork. To bake, close the pie maker until it locks then plug in the pie maker. The crust should bake for 11 to 12 minutes until crisp but not burnt. Unplug the pie maker. Completely cool the crusts on a wire cooling rack. Repeat the process until all the dough is used. For best results, fully cool the pie maker between each batch.

4. **To make the pies:** Fill the pie shells with 3 to 4 tablespoons of custard filling and smooth out the filling. The pies should be refrigerated for 15 to 20 minutes until the custard just sets. Smooth the raspberry jam with a whisk in a small bowl. On the top of each pie spread about 2 tablespoons of jam evenly. Top each pie with a fresh raspberry. The pie can be either served immediately or can be refrigerator until ready to serve.

5. For the best pie, eat as soon as possible; however, the pies will last in the refrigerator for up to 3 days if wrapped.

MINI CHOCOLATE PECAN PIES

Makes 12 mini pies.

EQUIPMENT
Muffin tin, 12 cup regular size
Medium bowl

INGREDIENTS
1 recipe double crust pie dough

¾ cup chopped pecans

36 cups pecan halves

¾ cup semisweet chocolate chips

3 eggs, beaten

⅓ cup granulated sugar

⅓ cup dark brown sugar

⅓ cup dark corn syrup

2 tablespoons Kahlúa or other coffee liqueur

½ teaspoon vanilla extract

⅛ teaspoon salt

COOKING INSTRUCTIONS

1. Preheat the oven to 325 degrees F.

2. Take the dough and divide it into 12 equal sections. Roll each section into a ball. Put each ball in a separate muffin cup. Press the ball into the muffin cup making sure to push the dough around the sides of the cup.

Using your fingertips, move the dough up to the top of the muffin cup.

3. Add 1 tablespoon chocolate chips and 1 tablespoon chopped pecans to each muffin cup. On top of the chopped pecans arrange 3 pecan halves.

4. Combine the eggs, granulated sugar, brown sugar, corn syrup, Kahlúa, vanilla and salt in a mixing bowl using a whisk. Coat all the pecans by pouring the filling over the nuts in the cup.

5. Bake until the filling sets and the crust is golden. This should take about 45 minutes. Take out of the oven and cool it in the pan for at least 30 minutes. Using a plastic knife, gently remove the pie from the pan. Keep pies in the refrigerator for up to 3 days.

Notes: The pies can keep in the freezer for about 2 months. Chill the pies first in the refrigerator. Wrap each pie separately with two layers of plastic wrap. Placed the wrapped pies into a freezer bag and transfer the bag to the freezer.

RUSTIC CHOCOLATE PIE

INGREDIENTS

¾ cup flour

¼ teaspoon salt

5 tablespoons cold unsalted butter

6 ounces bittersweet or semisweet chocolate, coarsely chopped

2 egg whites, at room temperature

⅛ teaspoon cream of tartar

½ teaspoon vanilla extract

¼ cup sugar

⅛ teaspoon salt

¾ cup chopped pecans, walnuts, or hazelnuts

3 tablespoons pine nuts, toasted

Chocolate shavings (optional)

COOKING INSTRUCTIONS

Crust:

1. Mix the flour and ¼ teaspoon salt in a mixing bowl. Add chunks of butter to the bowl. Using a fork or pastry blender, cut the butter into the flour. Toss the mixture until coated. The largest pieces will be the size of pine nuts. The butter should not be allowed to melt. Drizzle 1 ½ tablespoons cold water over the dough during the tossing. Mix the dough until it is moist enough to hold together when pressed. Use all the water if necessary. Place the dough on plastic wrap and form it into a disc.

The dough can be refrigerated for up to 3 days. Be sure to chill the dough for least 30 minutes before use.

2. Remove the dough from the refrigerator. Cool to room temperature for at least 30 minutes or until the dough can be rolled without cracking.

3. Preheat oven to 400 degrees F. Roll the dough out on a lightly floured surface. Once done you should create a 14 x 9 inch oval about ⅛ inch thick. You should dust the dough while rolling with flour and rotate the dough to prevent sticking. Dust off the extra flour from the dough. Fold the dough in half. Put the dough on a parchment paper lined baking sheet. Form a rimmed crust by loosely folding and roll the edge without pressing. Bake until the crust is a light golden brown for approximately 10 to 14 minutes. The crust may appear somewhat raw on the inside of the pan. Reduce the heat to 350 degrees F.

Filling:

1. Put the chocolate in a microwave safe bowl and cook in the microwave. Stop the microwave a few times to stir the chocolate. Once the chocolate is melted, set it aside.

2. Beat the egg whites, the cream of tartar and vanilla extract in a medium-sized bowl until soft peaks form. Slowly add in the sugar and ⅛ teaspoon salt. Beat until the whites are stiff but not dry. Add the nuts and melted chocolate over the whites. Using a spatula, fold the batter until it is a uniform color.

DESSERT RECIPES FOR CHOCOLATE LOVERS!

CHOCOLATE DECADENCE – OVER THE TOP DESSERTS

ESPRESSO TRUFFLE BROWNIES WITH ESPRESSO CHOCOLATE GANACHE AND WHIPPED CREAM

INGREDIENTS

1 cup unsalted butter, extra for greasing tin

1 tablespoon Dutch-process cocoa, extra for dusting tin

12 ounces good quality semi-sweet chocolate, finely chopped

¼ cup freshly brewed espresso

1 tablespoon pure vanilla extract

1 ¼ cups light brown sugar

4 large eggs

½ cup all-purpose flour

¼ teaspoon salt

½ cup walnuts, toasted, cooled and finely ground

1 cup good quality bittersweet or semi-sweet chocolate

COOKING INSTRUCTIONS

1. Preheat oven to 350 degrees F.

2. Grease a 2 x 8-inch square baking dish with butter and line with baking parchment.

3. Lightly dust some cocoa.

4. Melt chocolate on a double boiler under a low flame.

5. Blend together hot espresso, cocoa and vanilla until the ingredients are evenly dissolved.

6. Pour the espresso mixture into the chocolate and mix.

7. Stir in sugar and blend.

8. Add eggs one at a time beating after each addition until well combined to a smooth batter.

9. Sift together flour and salt and stir in to the chocolate mixture and mix until evenly incorporated.

10. Add ground nuts and stir.

11. Stir in chocolate chips, if preferred.

ESPRESSO CHOCOLATE GANACHE

INGREDIENTS

1 cup heavy whipping cream

4 teaspoons instant espresso powder

1 tablespoon golden corn syrup

10 ounces good quality bittersweet or semi-sweet chocolate, finely chopped

COOKING INSTRUCTIONS

1. Add chocolate to a heat proof bowl.

2. Add cream and espresso in a saucepan and heat over medium flame until espresso has melted and bubbles form.

3. Turn off heat and keep covered for 30 minutes.

4. Strain the coffee and add corn syrup.

5. Simmer over a medium flame until bubbles start forming on the sides of the pan and the corn syrup dissolves while stirring continuously.

6. Stirring the mixture add the chocolate and leave aside for 2 minutes.

7. Mix chocolate until it melts and the mixture is smooth using a spatula.

8. Pour over cooled brownies and leave at room temperature for 3 hours for the ganache to set.

WHIPPED CREAM TOPPING

INGREDIENTS
1 cup heavy cream
2 tablespoons powdered sugar, sifted
½ teaspoon vanilla extract

COOKING INSTRUCTIONS
1. Chill a large bowl, beater and cream.
2. Add cream, powdered sugar and vanilla into the bowl and beat using an electric hand mixer until soft peaks form
3. Chill until required.

To Serve Espresso Truffle Brownies:
Sweetened whipped cream, optional
Chocolate covered espresso beans, optional

1. Unmold brownie from tray and cut squares using a spatula dipped in hot water and wiped.
2. Fill whipped cream in a pastry bag with a plain tip and pipe per each piece of brownie and top it with an espresso bean.

DARK CHOCOLATE CUPCAKES WITH CHOCOLATE MASCARPONE BUTTERCREAM

INGREDIENTS

For the Cupcakes:

2 cups sugar

1¾ cups all-purpose flour

¾ cup Hershey's "Special Dark" Cocoa

1½ teaspoons baking powder

1½ teaspoons baking soda

1 teaspoon salt

2 eggs

1 cup milk

½ cup canola oil

2 teaspoons vanilla extract

1 cup boiling water or 1 cup hot brewed coffee

For the Mascarpone Buttercream:

4 ounces mascarpone cheese

½ cup butter, softened

⅓ cup Hershey's "Special Dark" Cocoa

2 tablespoons milk

2 teaspoons vanilla

16 ounce box powdered sugar, sifted

COOKING INSTRUCTIONS

Make the Cupcakes:

1. Preheat oven to 350 degrees F.

2. Line a muffin tray with paper cups.

3. In a large bowl, sift together flour, baking powder, baking soda and add salt with sugar and stir.

4. Beat in eggs, milk, oil and vanilla.

5. Beat on high speed using an electric hand mixer.

6. Pour boiling water or coffee and mix well.

7. Fill muffin pan with ⅔ of batter each and bake for 22 to 25 minutes.

8. Cool completely on a wire rack.

Make the Mascarpone Buttercream:

1. Add mascarpone cheese, butter, cocoa powder, milk and vanilla into a large mixing bowl and beat on high speed until the mixture is evenly incorporated.

2. Stir in powdered sugar and beat well to smooth mixture.

3. Stir in extra milk if necessary to acquire the consistency for cupcakes.

PEANUT BUTTER MARSHMALLOW-CRUNCH BROWNIES

INGREDIENTS

1 cup (2 sticks) unsalted butter, softened

2 cups light brown sugar

¾ cup Dutch-process cocoa powder

1 teaspoon salt

1 teaspoon baking powder

1 teaspoon espresso powder, optional

1 tablespoon vanilla

4 large eggs

1½ cups white whole wheat flour

2 cups semi-sweet chocolate chips

3 cups mini marshmallows

1 cup semi-sweet chocolate chips

1 cup smooth peanut butter

1½ cups bran buds cereal

COOKING INSTRUCTIONS

1. Preheat oven to 350 degrees F. Spray a 13 x 9-inch pan with cooking spray. If you like, you may line the pan with parchment paper or aluminum foil. Be sure that you leave an overhang on each end for easy removal after baking. It is helpful to spray the foil with cooking spray.

2. Put the butter in a microwave-safe bowl. Using a microwave, melt the butter. Stir in the brown sugar. Return the bowl to the microwave and heat until the mixture is warm and the sugar is more dissolved.

3. Put the butter mixture into a large bowl. Mix in the cocoa, salt, baking powder, espresso powder and vanilla. Add in 1 egg at a time. Be sure to stir after adding each egg to combine well. Finally, add the flour and chocolate chips. Mix the batter well to combine.

4. Pour the batter into the prepared pan. Bake for 25 minutes. Remove the pan from the oven and leave the oven on. Sprinkle the marshmallows evenly over the top of the brownies. Return to the oven for 5 minutes more. The marshmallows should be puffed and softened, but not browned. Remove pan from oven and allow to cool on a rack.

5. Heat the chocolate chips and peanut butter in a small microwave-safe bowl in the microwave, stirring frequently until the chips have melted and mixture is smooth. Add the bran buds and stir. Spoon out the mixture over the marshmallow-topped brownies. Spread evenly. The brownies should sit overnight before serving.

CHOCOLATE GELATO WITH HAZELNUT PRALINE

INGREDIENTS

Gelato:

1 cup granulated sugar

1 tablespoon corn syrup (optional)

2 cups whole milk, hot

¼ cup Dutch processed cocoa powder, sifted

3½ ounces fine-quality bittersweet chocolate (not unsweetened), chopped

4 large egg yolks, beaten lightly

1 cup hazelnuts, toasted and skinned, roughly chopped

Hazelnut Praline:

1 cup hazelnuts, toasted and skinned

⅔ cup granulated sugar

1 tablespoon corn syrup (optional)

COOKING INSTRUCTIONS

1. Melt ¼ cup sugar over medium heat until it melts without stirring and then stir with a fork until completely melted and turns golden brown in color and caramelized.

2. If preferred, add a teaspoon of corn syrup to avoid crystallizing the sugar.

3. Remove the pan from heat and place over a bowl of ice and cool for 5 minutes as the caramel hardens. Gently pour 2 ounces of milk at a time stirring constantly and carefully until all the milk is poured, cooking over medium flame until the caramel is melted well.

4. Stir in sifted cocoa and mix well, keeping the mixture warm.

5. Melt bittersweet chocolate on a double boiler stirring continuously, and leave aside.

6. If using a microwave, stir every 30 seconds until the entire chocolate is melted.

7. Beat egg yolks with ¾ cup of sugar using an electric mixer until thick and pale and stir in caramel mixture with chocolate part by part until the mixture is combined evenly.

8. Transfer the custard to a heavy bottomed sauce pan and cook over a low heat, stirring continuously until a candy thermometer inserted shows 140 degrees F., and make sure the mixture doesn't boil.

9. Cool the mixture at room temperature and over night in the fridge.

10. Freeze in your ice cream maker, following instructions in the manual, cover and freeze the churned gelato in a freezer container.

Praline:

1. Melt and cook sugar in a heavy bottomed pan until the edges start to melt without stirring.

2. Once the sugar melts, swirl pan and continue cooking until no crystals are left and the color turns golden brown in color.

3. Add 1 teaspoon of corn syrup if necessary to keep the sugar from crystallizing.

4. Spread hazelnuts on a pan lined with silicon mat and spoon the sugar syrup on top and cool completely before breaking the pralines.

5. Serve gelato garnished with pralines.

MISSISSIPPI MUDSLIDES

INGREDIENTS

2 pints chocolate ice cream

1 cup milk

½ cup bourbon, Kahlua, or Bailey's Irish Cream (optional)

Garnishes: Large marshmallows, whipped cream, chocolate syrup, chopped toasted pecans, and chocolate shavings.

COOKING INSTRUCTIONS

1. Blend together ice cream, milk and bourbon.

2. Pour equally into cups.

3. Top with 3 to 5 marshmallows on each cup and slightly brown the top of marshmallow using a torch.

4. Place a generous amount of whipped cream on top.

5. Garnish with chocolate syrup and sprinkle chopped pecans and chocolate shavings.

CHOCOLATE TORTE WITH COFFEE WHISKY MASCARPONE

INGREDIENTS

For the Chocolate Torte:

15 ounces unsalted butter

15 ounces dark chocolate, broken up

2 teaspoons vanilla extract

10 medium eggs

11 ounces superfine sugar

7 ounces pack ground almonds

3.75 ounces cocoa powder, sifted

For the Coffee Whiskey Mascarpone:

2 tablespoons instant espresso powder

6 tablespoons whiskey (or warm water if omitting the alcohol)

2 tablespoons icing sugar

17.75 ounces mascarpone

For the Chocolate Truffles:

7 ounces dark chocolate, chopped

2 ½ ounces double cream

1 teaspoon vanilla extract

Cocoa and grated white chocolate, for dusting

COOKING INSTRUCTIONS

1. Preheat oven to 350 degrees F.

2. Grease a round springform pan –10 inch diarmeter, approximately

3. Melt chocolate with butter on a double boiler and stir in vanilla extract.

4. Combine egg yolks with 4 ounces caster sugar and beat until the color turns pale.

5. Pour and mix egg mixture with the chocolate mixture.

6. Add almonds and cocoa powder.

7. Beat egg whites until stiff peaks form and add 7 ounces of caster sugar until evenly combined.

8. Add ⅓ of the egg whites to the chocolate mixture and combine.

9. Add the rest of egg whites and mix until evenly combined.

10. Evenly spread the mixture on to the baking pans and bake 45 minutes until done.

Truffle:
1. Melt chocolate, cream and vanilla in a pan.

2. Cool the melted chocolate and chill for 90 minutes or until set.

3. Once the mixture is set using an ice cream scooper or teaspoon make 12 truffles and dust cocoa powder and chill until the torte is ready.

Mascarpone cream:
1. Beat together espresso powder with whiskey and then add icing sugar and mascarpone in a separate bowl.

2. Mix well and leave aside.

3. Cool cake completely and slice into layers.

4. Spread mascarpone cream in between layer of cake and sandwich cakes.

5. Reheat rest of the ganache slightly and pour over the cake.

6. Use chocolate cream to secure truffles between torte.

7. Refrigerate the torte for 10 minutes and serve.

8. Sprinkle cocoa on top and serve.

EXTREME CHOCOLATE LOVER'S CAKE

INGREDIENTS

For the Cake:

2 ¼ cups all-purpose flour

2 teaspoons baking soda

½ teaspoon salt

6 (1 ounce) squares unsweetened chocolate, chopped

½ cup unsalted butter

2 ½ cups dark brown sugar

3 eggs

1 ½ tablespoons vanilla extract

1 cup sour cream

1 cup water

For the Chocolate Buttercream Frosting:

1 stick unsalted butter

⅔ cup unsweetened cocoa powder

3 cups powdered sugar

⅓ cup milk

1 teaspoon vanilla

For the Ganache:

2 cups bittersweet chocolate chips

1 cup heavy cream

COOKING INSTRUCTIONS

1. Preheat oven to 350 degrees F.

2. Butter and flour 2 round baking pans..

3. Melt 6 ounces of chocolate stirring continuously until smooth in a double boiler.

4. Cool melted chocolate completely.

5. Sift together flour, baking soda and salt.

6. In a large bowl beat together butter and brown sugar until fluffy.

7. Add eggs one at a time, beating continuously.

8. Add 1 ½ teaspoons vanilla and the melted chocolate and beat.

9. Add the 3 dry ingredients into the flour with the sour cream and beat until well incorporated.

10. Pour boiling water and mix.

11. Fill baking pans with ¾ batter and bake for 35-40 minutes.

12. Cool on the pan for 10 minutes before unmolding.

Chocolate Buttercream:

1. Beat butter in a separate bowl.

2. Add cocoa, powdered sugar, vanilla and little milk and mix well until evenly incorporated.

3. Add more milk until the mixture reaches a spreadable thick consistency.

Ganache:

1. Add chocolate chips with 1 cup cream into a large saucepan and melt, stirring continuously until the chocolate is melted and the mixture is smooth.

2. Assemble the cake

3. Cover the bottom cake with ganache and refrigerate for 5 minutes or until set. Place second cake on top.

4. Cover the top of cake with frosting and frost top and sides with buttercream and garnish with ganache if desired.

DOUBLE CHOCOLATE DIPPED STRAWBERRIES

INGREDIENTS

1 pound of large strawberries with stems

6 ounces dark chocolate

6 ounces white chocolate

INSTRUCTIONS

1. Wash the strawberries and completely dry. Make sure they are at room temperature.

2. Place waxed paper over a cookie sheet.

3. Melt the dark chocolate in a double boiler.

4. Holding the stem of strawberry, dip it into the melted chocolate. Turn to coat all sides. Shake to remove excess.

5. Lay the strawberry on the waxed paper. Repeat with the rest of the strawberries. Allow the chocolate to slightly harden.

6. Melt the white chocolate in a double boiler. Dip a fork in white chocolate and move back and forth over the chocolate strawberries to make a swirl design on both sides of each strawberry.

DESSERT RECIPES FOR CHOCOLATE LOVERS!

BROWNIES/BARS

ADULT BROWNIES

INGREDIENTS

2 tablespoons softened butter

2 tablespoons unsweetened cocoa powder

12 tablespoons unsalted butter, room temperature and cut up into cubes

2 - 4 ounce. bars high quality milk chocolate, coarsely chopped

2 - 4 ounce. bars high quality dark chocolate, coarsely chopped

¾ cup sugar

¾ cup light brown sugar

2 tablespoons vanilla extract

4 large eggs at room temperature

½ cup flour

1 teaspoon sea salt (NOT regular table salt)

1 tablespoon instant espresso powder

1- 4 ounce bar bittersweet chocolate, coarsely chopped

COOKING INSTRUCTIONS

1. Preheat the oven to 350 degrees F. Place the baking rack in the lower third of the oven.

2. Cut a piece of parchment paper into a rectangle that is 8 x 12 inches. Grease the top of the paper with 2 tablespoons of butter and then dust it with the 2 tablespoons of cocoa powder. Place the paper in an 8 x 8 inch baking pan. Allow the ends of the parchment to hang over the edge of the pan. (This will be the first of many times that you will need to wash chocolate off your hands during this recipe.)

3. In a large microwave safe bowl, add the milk and dark chocolate followed by the cubed butter. Microwave it at full power for 15 seconds. Take the bowl out of the oven and stir. Repeat this process 5 more times until the mixture is smooth. Let cool for 10 minutes.

4. Using a wooden spoon, add in both sugars and the vanilla to the chocolate and mix until well combined. Add the eggs in one at a time. Mix thoroughly after each egg until they are fully combined.

5. Next, add in the flour, the sea salt and the espresso powder to the chocolate mixture. With a hand mixer on medium high, beat until the batter is glossy and starts pulling away from the bowl. This should take 3 minutes. Using a wooden spoon, stir in the bittersweet chocolate.

6. Add the batter into the prepared pan. Bake for 45 minutes turning the pan ¼ turn twice during the baking. Poke the middle of the brownies with either a wooden skewer or toothpick. Continue baking until it comes out clean. Be sure to check the brownies at 5 minute intervals.

7. Cool the brownies in the pan on a rack for 15 minutes. Then remove the brownies from the pan carefully using the edges of the parchment paper to lift them from the pan. Cut into one-inch squares and serve.

TRIPLE CHOCOLATE CHIP TOPPED BROWNIES

INGREDIENTS

Brownie Layer:

6 ounces bittersweet chocolate

3 ounces unsweetened chocolate, coarsely chopped

2 sticks (8 ounces) unsalted butter, cut into chunks

1 ⅔ cups sugar

4 large eggs

½ teaspoon salt

½ teaspoon pure vanilla extract

1 cup all-purpose flour

1 cup walnuts, coarsely chopped

Cookie Layer:

1 ¼ cups all-purpose flour

½ teaspoon baking soda

½ teaspoon salt

1 ½ sticks (12 tablespoons) unsalted butter, at room temperature

¾ cup (packed) light brown sugar

⅔ cup sugar

1 large egg

1 large egg yolk

1 teaspoon pure vanilla extract

6 ounces bittersweet chocolate, chopped into chips, or 1 cup store-bought chocolate chips

COOKING INSTRUCTIONS

1. Place a rack in the center of the oven. Preheat the oven to 350 degrees F. Butter the bottom of a 9 × 13-inch baking pan, line it with parchment paper and then butter the top of the paper. Put the pan on a baking sheet.

2. To make the brownie batter, put both chocolates and the butter in a glass or metal bowl. Set the bowl over a saucepan of simmering water. Stir occasionally. Be sure to only heat until the ingredients are melted, shiny and smooth. Remove the bowl from the heat. You can also microwave the chocolates and butter together in 30-second increments. Be sure to stir well after each increment.

3. You can beat the sugar and eggs with either a stand mixer fitted with a paddle attachment or using a hand mixer in a large bowl for 2 minutes. The mix will be pale, thick and creamy. Next, add in the salt and vanilla extract and mix. With the mixer on low speed, add in the melted chocolate and butter. Be sure to mix only until incorporated. Use a rubber spatula to scrape the sides of the bowl. Still on low speed, use a mixer to add the flour. Mix only until the flour disappears into the batter. Fold in the walnuts with a spatula. Next, scrape out the batter and add it into the prepared pan. Set aside the pan.

4. With a whisk, mix together the flour, baking soda and salt to make the cookie dough.

5. In a stand mixer with a cleaned bowl or with the hand mixer in another large bowl on medium-high speed, beat the butter and both sugars together until smooth and creamy for about 3 minutes. Add in the egg and the yolk one at a time. Beat for 1 minute after each addition. Next beat in the vanilla. With the mixer on low, add the dry ingredients. Mix only until the dry ingredients disappear into the dough. Next, mix in the chopped chocolate, continuing with the mixer on low. Spoon out drops of cookie dough over the brownie batter. Use a spatula and lightly spread it evenly over the batter.

6. Place the pan into the oven and bake for 50 to 55 minutes. The cookie top should be golden brown and firm. A thin knife cut into the brownie layer comes out with only faint streaks of moist chocolate. Once done, put the pan on a rack and cool it to room temperature.

7. After the brownies are cooled take a knife and run it carefully between the sides of the pan and the brownies. Flip the brownies onto another rack. Remove the parchment paper and then turn the brownies right side up onto a cutting board. Cut the brownies into bars about 2 inches by 1 inch.

TRUFFLE BROWNIES

INGREDIENTS

4 tablespoons unsalted butter

3 ounces semi-sweet chocolate, chopped

½ cup unbleached all-purpose flour

¼ teaspoon baking powder

½ teaspoon salt

¾ cup sugar

2 eggs, room temperature

¼ cup milk

1 teaspoon pure vanilla extract

2 ounces semi-sweet chocolate, chopped

⅓ cup heavy cream

COOKING INSTRUCTIONS

1. Preheat oven to 325 degrees F. Use cooking spray to grease a 9-inch round springform pan, making sure you really spray the bottom. Set the pan aside.

2. Set a glass or metal bowl over a pot of simmering water. Add butter and semi-sweet chocolate into the bowl. Be sure to stir until the butter and chocolate have melted together. Remove from the pot and set aside to cool slightly.

3. Using a whisk, mix together the flour, baking powder and salt in a small bowl. Set the bowl aside. In a large bowl, use a whisk to mix the sugar and eggs until pale

and fluffy. Add the chocolate mixture to the large bowl. Stir until well combined. Next, mix in the milk and vanilla. Add the flour mixture into the large bowl. Stir until well incorporated.

4. Add the batter into the prepared pan. Set the pan onto the middle rack of the oven. Bake for 25 to 27 minutes or until a toothpick inserted comes out clean with the exception of a few crumbs. Allow the brownies to cool on the counter while you make the ganache.

5. Put the chocolate into a small bowl. Add the cream into a saucepan over a medium heat until simmering. Pour the cream over the chocolate. Let sit for about 5 minutes. Lightly stir until smooth. Allow the ganache to cool. Stir every 10 minutes until thickens.

6. Pour ganache over cooled brownies that are still in the pan. Put the pan in refrigerater for about 30 minutes until chilled. Remove from the refrigerator and use a paring knife around the edges of the cake pan. Remove the bottom of the cake pan. Cut the brownies into wedges.

CARAMEL BROWNIES

Yield: 24+ brownies

INGREDIENTS:

1 cup (2 sticks) unsalted butter

12 ounces bittersweet chocolate, coarsely chopped

1 ½ cups sugar

4 large eggs

1 tablespoon vanilla extract

1 ¼ cups all-purpose flour

½ teaspoon salt

1 ½ cups pecan, coarsely chopped (optional)

1 cup semi-sweet chocolate chips

Caramel filling:

14 ounces caramel candies, unwrapped

⅓ cup heavy cream

COOKING INSTRUCTIONS

1. Preheat the oven to 350 degrees F. Line a 9 x 13-inch baking pan with foil. Use butter or cooking spray to grease the foil well. In a metal or glass bowl, combine the butter and chocolate. Place the bowl over a pan of simmering water. Completely melt the mixture until smooth, stirring occasionally. (You can perform the process in the microwave. Heat the mixture for 30 seconds at a time. Stir between each interval. Repeat until the mixture is completely melted.) Remove the bowl from the heat. Using

a whisk, mix in the sugar, eggs and vanilla until well combined. Stir in the flour and salt just until combined. Spread about half of the brownie batter in the bottom of the prepared pan. Spread evenly. Bake for 20 minutes. Remove from the oven and allow to cool for 20 minutes. Do not turn off the oven.

2. While the brownies are cooking, add the optional chopped pecans to a medium skillet. Toast the pecans over medium heat, stirring occasionally until fragrant and a light golden brown. Remove from the stove and set aside.

To make the caramel filling: In a medium saucepan over a medium-low heat combine the caramel candies and cream. Stir the caramels and cream frequently until melted and smooth. Add in half of the pecans. Once combined, immediately spread the caramel mixture over the bottom layer of brownies. Over the layer of caramel, add the remaining brownie batter. Be sure to spread the batter evenly. If the batter is not evenly spread it will be difficult to spread evenly over the caramel layer. Over the top layer of brownies, sprinkle the chocolate chips and the remaining pecans. Bake for 20 minutes. Transfer the pan to a wire rack to let cool completely. (To speed the cooling, the brownies can be chilled in the freezer for at least 30 minutes.)

3. Take the brownies out of the pan using the edges of the foil. Remove the foil and cut the brownies into individual squares. Store the brownies in an airtight container.

MEXICAN HOT CHOCOLATE BROWNIES

Yield: 16 brownies

INGREDIENTS

4 ounces. unsweetened chocolate, roughly chopped

6 tablespoons butter

¾ cup granulated sugar

¼ cup packed light brown sugar

2 large eggs

1 teaspoon pure vanilla extract

⅓ cup plus 1 tablespoon all-purpose flour

½ teaspoon ground cinnamon

¼ teaspoon ground cayenne pepper

Pinch of ground cloves

¼ teaspoon salt

2 tablespoons raw cacao nibs for topping

COOKING INSTRUCTIONS

1. Preheat the oven to 350 degrees F. Put the rack in the center position of the oven. Line an 8 x 8 inch square metal baking pan with parchment paper. Be sure to leave two inches on both ends.

2. In a large heat proof bowl place the chocolate and butter. Set the bowl over a pot with ½-inch of simmering water over medium-low heat. Using a whisk, gently mix the chocolate and butter until completely melted, smooth and glossy. Turn off the heat under the pot.

Leave the bowl over the pot and whisk in both sugars until blended evenly. Remove the bowl from the heat. Cool the bowl for three minutes. Using a whisk, mix in the eggs, one at a time. Mix vigorously for about 10 seconds to combine each egg before adding the next egg. The batter should be smooth and shiny. Finally, whisk in vanilla extract.

3. Using a rubber spatula, add the flour, spices and salt. Stir until blended and smooth.

4. Scrape the batter from the bowl using the spatula into the prepared pan. Spread the batter into the corners evenly. Sprinkle cocoa nibs over top of the batter. Bake about 23 to 25 minutes. Take care not to over bake. A skewer or toothpick put into the center of the brownie should come out with a few moist crumbs. Transfer to a wire rack and cool completely in the pan.

CHOCOLATE STOUT BROWNIES

Yield: 16 to 20 brownies

INGREDIENTS

1 cup chocolate stout

16 ounces semi-sweet chocolate, divided (I used two boxes of Baker's semisweet chocolate, which contain 8 ounces each)

1 cup plus 2 tablespoons unsalted butter, softened

1½ cups sugar

3 large eggs

1 teaspoon vanilla extract

¾ cup all-purpose flour

1½ teaspoons salt, divided

COOKING INSTRUCTIONS

1. Preheat oven to 350 degrees F. Use foil to line a 9 x 9 x 2-inch square non-stick baking pan. Be sure to leave a two inch overhang on each end to allow you to lift the brownies out of the pan later. Spray the foil with non-stick cooking spray.

2. Bring the chocolate stout over a medium saucepan to a boil. Let simmer for about 10 minutes until reduced to ½ cup. You can easily check how much of the stout is left by pouring the liquid into a glass measuring cup. Transfer the liquid back to continue simmering, if the temperature has not gotten high enough. When

reduced, remove from heat and let cool. Divide stout into two ¼ cup measurements. You will use half in the brownie batter and half in the glaze.

3. In a medium metal bowl, combine chopped 12 ounces of chocolate and 1 cup butter cut into pieces. Put the bowl over a small saucepan with simmering water in it. Stir the chocolate and butter until smooth and melted. Remove the bowl from heat.

4. Using a whisk, mix the sugar, eggs and vanilla in a large bowl until smooth. Slowly whisk in the melted chocolate mixture and ¼ cup of the reduced stout. Lightly fold in the flour and 1 and ¼ teaspoons salt. In the prepared pan pour the batter.

5. Bake brownies for 40 to 50 minutes until the surface begins to crack. A tester toothpick inserted into the center of the pan should come out with a few moist crumbs when done. Remove from oven and transfer them to a wire rack. Let cool in the pan for at least 20 minutes.

6. **To make the glaze:** Simmer water in a small saucepan. In a medium bowl add the remaining 4 ounces of chocolate and place over the saucepan. Stir the chocolate until melted and smooth. Remove the bowl from the heat. Add in the rest of the reduced stout, 2 tablespoons of butter and ¼ teaspoon of salt and whisk until well blended.

7. Use the warm glaze to pour over the brownies. Let stand for at least 40 minutes at room temperature until the glaze sets. Use the foil edges to lift the brownies out of the pan. Cut the brownies into small squares. These brownies are very rich so you may not want the pieces to be too big.

BOURBON BROWNIES

Yield: 20 small brownies

INGREDIENTS

¼ cup bourbon

¼ cup bittersweet chocolate chips

1 ½ cups all-purpose flour

½ cup unsweetened cocoa

1 teaspoon baking powder

½ teaspoon salt

1 ⅓ cups sugar

6 tablespoons butter, softened

½ teaspoon vanilla extract

2 large eggs

Cooking spray

COOKING INSTRUCTIONS

1. Preheat the oven to 350 degrees F. Prepare a 9-inch square baking pan coated with cooking spray.

2. In a small saucepan, bring the bourbon to a boil. Remove the bourbon from heat. Add in the chocolate chips and stir until smooth.

3. Using a whisk, mix the flour, cocoa, baking powder, and salt until combined.

4. In a large bowl, beat the sugar and butter with a mixer at medium speed until well combined. Add in the vanilla and eggs and beat well. Mix in the flour mixture and bourbon mixture to the sugar mixture. Beat with the mixer at a low speed until just combined.

5. Spread batter into the prepared pan. Bake for 25 minutes. Use a wooden pick to check if done. When inserted in the center the wooden pick should come out clean. Cool in pan on wire rack.

ROCKY ROAD

INGREDIENTS

3.75 ounces unsalted butter

8 ounces. dark chocolate

2 ounces Rice Krispies

6 ½ ounces marshmallows

2 ½ ounces pistachio nuts, toasted

5 ounces raspberry puree

COOKING INSTRUCTIONS

1. In a double boiler melt dark chocolate and butter, stirring continuously.

2. If you don't have a double boiler, fill a sauce pan with water and boil.

3. On top of the sauce pan place a heat proof bowl and add the chocolate with butter, and melt on a medium flame.

4. Once the chocolate is melted cool at room temperature, stirring occasionally.

5. In a separate bowl, combine the Rice Kripies, marshmallows, pistachio nuts and raspberries.

6. Add Rice Krispees, marshmallows, pistachio nuts and raspberries in a separate bowl and pour the chocolate

mixture on top of the raspberries mixture and gently combine to spread evenly.

7. Line a large baking tray sides and bottom with baking paper and spread the mixture, evenly pressing down the top to form a firm block.

8. Place another sheet of baking parchment on top of the rocky road mixture and place an equal size baking tray on top of the parchment with a heavy weight on the baking tray.

9. Refrigerate the mixture until firm for 1 to 2 hours.

10. Lift the baking parchment of the rocky road and place on a chopping board and slice small blocks using a serrated bread knife.

ICE CREAM, GELATO, AND SORBET

RIDICULOUSLY RICH DARK CHOCOLATE SORBET

INGREDIENTS

2 ¼ cups water

1 cup white sugar

¾ cup cocoa powder – Dutch processed (This has been treated with alkali to neutralize the natural acids, darker in color and slightly different in flavor from natural cocoa.)

¼ teaspoon salt

½ teaspoon vanilla extracts

3.75 ounces dark chocolate – 70% cocoa, chopped

TIP: Break the chocolate up as much as possible while it's still unopened then open the package and cut the chocolate up with a knife within the wrapping – no mess, no fuss!

COOKING INSTRUCTIONS

1. Add water, sugar, cocoa powder and salt into a large pan and mix altogether and bring to a boil over a medium heat, stirring continuously.

2. Turn off the heat and add chopped chocolates with vanilla and stir well until the chocolate melts.

3. Let the mixture cool and refrigerate to 35 degrees F.

4. Follow instructions in your ice cream maker and pour the ice cream mixture you refrigerated into the ice cream maker, once the ice cream is ready, transfer into a pre-chilled container and freeze.

CHOCOLATE ICE CREAM

INGREDIENTS

7 ounces dark chocolate (70% to 75% cacao), finely chopped

2 cups plus 2 tablespoons whole milk

⅓ cup unsweetened cocoa powder

6 large egg yolks

13 tablespoons sugar, divided

¼ cup heavy whipping cream

COOKING INSTRUCTIONS

1. Over a double boiler melt chocolate and set aside to cool slightly.

2. In a medium sauce pan over a medium flame add milk and cocoa, whisk continuously until the mixture starts boiling.

3. Beat egg yolks with 7 tablespoons of sugar with an electric mixer until the mixture thickens.

4. Add hot milk and whisk continuously.

5. Transfer the egg yolk into a pan with melted chocolate and blend.

6. Cook the mixture over a very low flame until the mixture thickens slightly and a thermometer inserted displays 175 degrees.

7. Pour the chocolate custard into a large bowl and cool over another bowl filled with ice water.

8. Mix 6 tablespoons sugar and 2 tablespoons water in a heavy bottom pan and boil over a medium-high heat until sugar dissolves and the syrup turns dark amber color while being swirled in the pan. (Do not stir)

9. Pour in cream mixture, whisking continuously.

10. Blend caramel mixture with chocolate custard and strain into a container.

11. Cover and freeze for 2 days.

12. Whisk caramel into chocolate custard. Strain into a large container and freeze for 2 days.

13. Pour the mixture into an ice cream maker and process according to instructions.

14. Pour the ice cream into a container and freeze for 3 more days.

15. Keep frozen.

ROCKY ROAD ICE CREAM

INGREDIENTS

2 cups heavy cream, divided

3 tablespoons cocoa powder

5 ounces semi-sweet chocolate, finely chopped

1 cup whole milk

¾ cup sugar

Pinch of salt

5 large egg yolks

½ teaspoon vanilla extract

1 ½ cups miniature marshmallows

1 cup honey roasted peanuts, coarsely chopped

COOKING INSTRUCTIONS

1. Mix together a cup of heavy cream and cocoa powder in a medium sauce pan.

2. Warm the cocoa and cream mixture over a medium high flame, stirring continuously until cocoa dissolves.

3. Let the mixture boil once after the cocoa is dissolved and reduce the flame.

4. Stirring continuously, reduce heat to medium low and let it simmer for a second.

5. Take off heat and stir in chocolates and beat until the Chocolate melts and the mixture is smooth.

6. Pour the other cup of the cream and combine evenly.

7. Pour the contents into a mixing bowl and cover with a fine mesh sieve.

8. Warm the milk, sugar and salt in the same pan over medium heat .

9. Whisk 5 egg yolks in a separate bowl and add the milk mixture, stirring continuously soon after the milk starts warming.

10. Heat the egg and milk mixture over a medium high heat in a medium sauce pan, stirring continuously until the mixture thickens and the right consistency is achieved.

11. Transfer the custard through the fine sieve on top of the chocolate mixture and stir in some vanilla essence.

12. Cover and refrigerate for at least 3 to 4 hours.

13. Freeze the mixture in an ice cream maker. Follow instructions in your ice cream makers manual.

14. Combine the mini-marshmallows and peanuts, mixing evenly.

15. Freeze ice cream in an airtight box for a few hours until firm and ready to serve.

SPICY CHOCOLATE ICE CREAM

INGREDIENTS

- 2 ¼ cups heavy cream
- 6 tablespoons cocoa powder
- 5 ounces brown sugar
- 3 star anise pods
- 3 ouncesdark chocolate, chopped
- 1 ¼ cups whole milk
- 1 teaspoon vanilla extract
- Pinch of salt
- 1 ¼ teaspoons ground cinnamon
- ½ teaspoon cayenne pepper (see note)
- 2 tablespoons brandy

COOKING INSTRUCTIONS

1. Add heavy cream, cocoa, brown sugar and star anise into a medium saucepan and boil over a medium heat, stirring continuously until the mixture is blended together to a smooth and rolling consistency.

2. Add chocolate off the flame and beat until the chocolate melts.

3. Remove the star anise pods and add whole milk with vanilla, salt, cinnamon, and brandy.

4. Blend the ice cream base until smooth using a blender.

5. Refrigerate the mixture for minimum of 4 hours or overnight.

6. Transfer the contents to an ice cream maker and freeze according to instructions in your machine for 4 hours.

7. Line a sheet of plastic or parchment on top to prevent ice forming.

8. Adjust the pepper according to your preference. Add a quarter teaspoon at a time while whisking and tasting until the required level is reached. **Note:** The spiciness will increase as it cools.

SICILIAN CHOCOLATE GELATO WITH BOURBON AND DARK CHOCOLATE CHIPS

Note: Sicilian gelato is light and refreshing yet with good ingredients. It's also a very satisfyingly rich dessert.

INGREDIENTS

3 cups whole milk

¼ cup half and half

⅔ cup granulated sugar

¾ cup Unsweetened Natural Cocoa Powder

1½ tablespoons cornstarch

¼ cup bourbon

¼ to ½ cup chopped chocolate or chocolate chips

COOKING INSTRUCTIONS

1. Heat 2 cups of milk in a medium pan.

2. Mix together sugar, cocoa, cornstarch and pour in the other cup of milk with half and half.

3. Add scraped coconut to the cocoa mixture and cook, stirring continuously until the mixture thickens and forms slight bubbles. Stir and cook for 2 more minutes.

4. Remove from heat and add and mix the bourbon.

5. Transfer the contents into a clean bowl and cover top with a plastic wrap and chill until the mixture is cold, or freeze for 45 minutes to chill it faster.

6. Freeze the ice cream in your ice cream maker according to your machine's instructions; it may take less than suggested in your ice cream maker as the ice cream mixture is thick.

7. Stir in chocolate chips and give it a quick mix.

8. Transfer ice cream into a container and freeze for 4 hours and serve.

CHOCOLATE MINT STOUT ICE CREAM

INGREDIENTS

2 cups whole milk

3 fresh mint leaves

1 cup heavy cream

1 cup chocolate stout, or chocolate mint stout

7 ounces of 60% dark chocolate with peppermint oil (such as Dark Chocolate Mint from Green & Blacks), broken into chunks

4 egg yolks

1 ¼ cup white sugar

COOKING INSTRUCTIONS

1. In a pan add milk, mint leaves, cream and stout. Cook over a medium high heat and bring to a simmer.

2. Remove from heat and take the mint leaves and stir in chocolates until melted.

3. Add egg yolks with sugar into a bowl and beat well.

4. Gently add chocolate milk and stir continuously until half the mixture is evenly incorporated to the egg yolks.

5. Transfer the egg yolk mixture back into the pot and beat until mixed evenly and heat until the mixture reaches to a low simmer.

6. Chill for 3 hours and churn in the ice cream maker, following the instructions in the manual until firm.

MILK CHOCOLATE ICE CREAM WITH BROWNIE BITS

INGREDIENTS

For the Brownies:

8 tablespoons unsalted butter, cut into pieces

4 ounces unsweetened chocolate, chopped

1 ¼ cups sugar

2 large eggs

1 teaspoon vanilla extract

½ cup all-purpose flour

Pinch of salt

½ cup semi-sweet or bittersweet chocolate chips

For the Ice Cream:

8 ounces milk chocolate (at least 30% cacao solids), finely chopped

1 ½ cups heavy cream

1 ½ cups whole milk

¾ cup sugar

Pinch of salt

4 large egg yolks

COOKING INSTRUCTIONS

1. Preheat oven to 350 degrees F and line an 8 x 8 inch baking tray with aluminum foil with nonstick spray.

2. Melt butter in a small pan.

3. Stir hoped Choctaws until melted and remove from heat and beat in sugar, eggs and vanilla.

4. Combine flour, salt and fold in chocolate chips gently.

5. Spread batter on the baking tray and bake for 30 minutes until firm.

6. Cool completely and cut half the brownies into small bits, which can be mixed with the ice cream.

7. Double boil milk, chocolate and heavy cream, stirring occasionally until the chocolate is melted.

8. Once the mixture is smooth take off heat and place a mesh sieve on top of the bowl and leave aside.

9. Heat milk, sugar and salt in a saucepan over a medium flame until the sugar dissolve.

10. Beat egg yolks in a medium mixing bowl and gently stir in warm milk mixture to the egg yolks and mix.

11. Pour the mixture back to the pan and cool stirring, continuously until the mixture is thick and smooth coating a spoon.

12. An instant read thermometer inserted should indicate 170-175 degrees F.

13. Turn off heat and pour the mixture through the sieve into the chocolate mixture.

14. Chill covered.

15. Freeze the ice cream mixture in an ice cream maker, following instructions in the manual.

16. Gently mix brownie bits with ice cream using a spatula and freeze covered.

CHOCOLATE ICE CREAM SANDWICHES

INGREDIENTS

The Praline:

3.75 ounces slivered almonds

3.75 ounces caster sugar

The Biscuits:

4 ½ ounces unsalted butter, chopped

2 ½ ounces caster sugar

2 ½ ounces praline, ground

5 ounces plain flour

½ ounces cocoa powder

½ teaspoon bicarbonate of soda

¼ teaspoon salt

The Ice Cream:

3 cups of whole milk

11 ounces cream

1 ounces skimmed milk powder

3.75 ounces caster sugar

10 large eggs free-range egg yolks

11 ounces good quality dark chocolate, roughly chopped

COOKING INSTRUCTIONS

The Praline:

1. Heat a heavy bottom sauce pan over medium heat.
2. Divide the sugar into three and add ⅓ into the pan and melt.
3. Add another ⅓ and melt.
4. Lastly, add the remaining ⅓ and melt.
5. Do not stir.
6. Cook until the caramel turn's dark and tie in almonds.
7. Spread over the baking tray lined with baking parchment.
8. Bake praline and break into large pieces.
9. Process to fine crumbs in a food processor.

The Biscuits:

1. Preheat oven at 375 degrees F
2. Cream butter, sugar and praline until light and fluffy.
3. Combine flour, cocoa, bicarbonate soda and salt.
4. Gently add to the butter mixture and beat on low until the mixture forms a ball.

5. Spread heaped tablespoon of cookie dough on a baking tray lined with baking parchment and bake for 15 minutes.

6. Cool biscuits completely and store in air tight containers.

The Ice Cream:

1. Add milk and cream to a heavy bottomed saucepan.

2. Over a medium flame, stir in skimmed milk powder with a tablespoon of sugar and take off before it boils.

3. Beat egg yolks with remaining sugar using an electric mixer on full speed for about 10 minutes.

4. As the cream mixture reaches a boiling point gently mix half with the egg mixture, stirring continuously.

5. Cook the custard over a low heat until the mixture reaches 83 degrees F, stirring continuously.

6. Make sure the mixture doesn't boil.

7. Turn off heat and stir in chocolate. Mix until chocolate melts.

8. Strain the mixture through a sieve onto a bowl placed on top of a large bowl filled with ice and cool the mixture stir every 2 minutes.

9. Refrigerate for 24 hours.

10. Line several 3 inch diameter ring molds lined with non-stick paper

11. Pour chilled cream anglaise in an ice cream maker and churn following instructions in your ice cream maker.

12. Once done, pour the ice cream into the ring molds and freeze completely.

TO ASSEMBLE:

1. Unmold the ice cream and sandwich a ring of ice cream between two biscuits. Freeze before serving.

2. You can even dip biscuits in ice cream and eat as it is or with salted caramel sauce.

TIN ROOF ICE CREAM CAKE

INGREDIENTS

7 tablespoons unsalted butter melted

Parchment or waxed paper

8 ounces chocolate wafer cookies

For the Ganache:

8 ounces bittersweet chocolate, coarsely chopped

1 cup heavy cream

2 tablespoons unsalted butter, cut into small pieces

For the Assembly:

2 quarts (4 pints) peanut butter ice cream, softened

1 cup chilled heavy cream, for garnish

Unsweetened cocoa powder, for garnish

A few handfuls roasted salted peanuts, roughly chopped, for garnish

1 ounce bittersweet chocolate, finely chopped, for garnish

COOKING INSTRUCTIONS

For the Crust:

1. Using a pastry brush, coat the inside of a 9-inch springform pan with 1 tablespoon of the melted butter. Cut parchment or waxed paper into a circle the same size as the base of the pan and place it in the base.

2. Place cookies in the bowl of a food processor and pulse until ground; add remaining 6 tablespoons melted

butter and pulse until mixture is moistened. Press mixture evenly and firmly into the bottom of the prepared pan and freeze until it's good and set, about 30 minutes. Meanwhile, take the ice cream out of the freezer to soften and make the ganache.

For the Ganache:

1. Place chocolate in a medium heatproof bowl; set aside. Place cream in a small saucepan over medium heat and bring to a simmer. Pour cream over chocolate and let stand until chocolate has melted, about 5 minutes.

2. Stir gently until smooth then stir in butter, one piece at a time, until completely incorporated; let cool slightly before using. Meanwhile, let the ice cream soften, for another 15 minutes or until soft enough to spread like room temperature butter, but not melted.

Assemble:

1. When ice cream is softened, transfer to a mixing bowl. Using a rubber spatula, mix until spreadable. Spread half of the ice cream over the cookie crust and smooth the top. Pour half of the ganache over the top and smooth and place in the freezer until firm, at least 30 minutes. Place the remaining ice cream back in the freezer, as well.

2. Remove peanut butter ice cream from the freezer and let soften about 15 minutes. Mix again until spreadable. Spread peanut butter ice cream over the fudge, level the top of the cake, add remaining ganache (you may want

to reheat this slightly until it's just pourable), smooth it, and freeze until the whole cake is very firm, at least 3 hours or up to 1 day.

TIP: Dip a large knife in hot water, wipe dry, and run around the rim of the pan to loosen ice cream from the sides; repeat as necessary.

To Serve:

1. Remove cake from the freezer and let sit a few minutes at room temperature before cutting. Meanwhile, place whipped cream in a clean, large bowl and whip with a whisk until soft peaks form.

2. Top cake with whipped cream, cocoa, peanuts, chocolate shavings, and serve.

CHOCOLATE OBSESSION CAKE

INGREDIENTS

For cake:

2 sticks butter

1 cup water

½ cup cocoa

2 cups sugar

2 cups all-purpose flour

2 large eggs

½ cup buttermilk

1 teaspoon salt

1 ½ teaspoons baking soda

1 tablespoon vanilla

COOKING INSTRUCTIONS

Cake:

1. Preheat oven to 350 degrees F.

2. Coat a baking pan of choice using baking spray.

3. Add butter, water and cocoa into a microwave safe dish and microwave for 3 minutes. Stir once after 1 and a half minutes.

4. Stir in sugar and flour, mix until smooth.

5. Beat in eggs with buttermilk, salt, soda and vanilla.

6. Spread batter evenly into buttered and flowered cake tins, and bake 25 to 30 minutes in an 11 x 15-inch pan.

7. If using muffin pans, bake 15 to 25 minutes.

8. Once the cake is baked, cool on a wire rack before frosting.

CHOCOLATE OBSESSION FROSTING

INGREDIENTS
1 stick butter
4 ounces unsweetened baking chocolate
½ cup milk
4 cups powdered sugar, approximately
1 teaspoon vanilla

FROSTING INSTRUCTIONS:

1. Microwave butter with baking chocolate in high for 1 ½ minutes in a microwave safe bowl.

2. Using a hand whisk or blender, blend the melted chocolate and stir in milk with vanilla until smooth.

3. The frosting should be thick and slightly warm in a pourable consistency. If the mixture is too thin add some powdered sugar.

4. Pour the warm frosting over the cake using an offset knife, spreading evenly. Cool before cutting.

5. For individual cupcakes, divide frosting equally and spread over the cupcakes.

CHOCOLATE WASTED CAKE

INGREDIENTS

For Cake:

3 cups all-purpose flour

2 ½ cups sugar

1 cup cocoa powder

2 teaspoons baking soda

1 teaspoon salt

2 cups milk

1 cup butter, melted

4 teaspoons honey

2 teaspoons vanilla extract

½ cup semi-sweet chocolate chips

Frosting:

4 cups powdered sugar, sifted

1 cup cocoa powder

½ cup butter, softened to room temperature

⅓ to ½ cup whole milk (start out with ⅓ cup of milk and add more to your desired consistency)

1 teaspoon vanilla extract

Liqueur for drizzling on the cake layers (i.e. chocolate, coffee or almond)

Melted chocolate for drizzling

2 cups semi-sweet chocolate chips

½ cup heavy cream or ¼ cup vegetable oil

Semi-sweet, bittersweet or dark chocolate chips for the sides of the cake

Assorted chocolate candies for the top of the cake

COOKING INSTRUCTIONS

(**Note:** Instead of milk, you can replace it with water or cooled brewed coffee. Instead of butter, you can use vegetable oil. Instead of honey, you can use corn syrup or agave nectar. Instead of semi-sweet chocolate chips, you can use Enjoy Life brand chocolate chips.* For allergen-free alternatives for the candies, you can try Enjoy Life chocolate chips, bars or cookies)

1. Preheat oven to 325 to 350 degrees F.

2. Grease an 8 or 9 inch cake pan with flour and line it with baking parchment.

3. Sift flour, sugar, cocoa powder, baking soda and salt together.

4. Combine milk, butter, honey and vanilla extract in a separate mixing bowl.

5. Gently stir in dry ingredients with the wet ingredients and mix evenly.

6. Stir in chocolate chips and spread cake mixture into the cake pan and bake for 30 to 45 minutes.

7. Cool on the baking tray for 10 minutes before removing and cool completely before frosting.

TO MAKE THE FROSTING:

1. Sift together powdered sugar and cocoa powder.

2. Add butter, milk and vanilla to a medium mixing bowl.

3. Beat wet and dry ingredients together using an electric beater on low and increase speed as the mixture is combined evenly and fluffy.

TO ASSEMBLE THE CAKE:

1. Pour some liqueur over the cake layer to soak slightly and spread frosting evenly.

2. Place the other cake on top of the frosting and drizzle with some liqueur on top. Apply frosting on top and all around the cake to cover.

3. Sprinkle and cover the cake with semi-sweet chocolate chips and candies.

4. Pour melted chocolate on top, letting it drip on the sides.

DESSERT RECIPES FOR CHOCOLATE LOVERS!

CHOCOLATE VANILLA FROZEN CAKE

INGREDIENTS

Moist Chocolate Cake:

1 and ¾ cups

1 and ⅓ cups

¾ cup unsweetened cocoa powder

1 teaspoon baking powder

1 pinch of salt

2 eggs

4/5 cup buttermilk

1 stick butter, melted

4/5 cup freshly brewed hot coffee

Ice Cream Filling:

1 quart vanilla ice-cream

Chocolate Frosting:

4/5 cup heavy cream

½ stick butter

9 ounces dark chocolate

Chopped almonds to decorate

COOKING INSTRUCTIONS

1. Preheat oven to 350 degrees F

2. Dust two 9 inch baking pans with flour

3. Sift flour, sugar, cocoa, baking soda and salt together.

4. Add eggs, buttermilk, melted butter and vanilla extract and beat until smooth

5. In a mixing bowl, add eggs, buttermilk, and melted butter, and vanilla. Beat until smooth and add warm coffee and the dry ingredients. Mix well until combined evenly.

6. Pour the batter into the cake pans evenly and bake for 20 to 25 minutes on the middle rack of oven.

7. Leave cake in the pan for 15 minutes before unmolding.

8. Cool cakes completely on a wire rack.

9. Line a mold pan with parchment paper.

10. Leave ice cream out of freezer for a few minutes.

11. Boil cream in a medium saucepan and stir in chopped chocolate with butter.

12. Leave a few minutes and stir until dissolved.

13. Pour the frosting over the cake evenly and sprinkle some chopped almonds. Freeze until time to serve.

DESSERT RECIPES FOR CHOCOLATE LOVERS!

MOUSSE

CHOCOLATE ESPRESSO MOUSSE

INGREDIENTS

- 7 ounces dark chocolate
- 4 tablespoons unsalted butter
- ¼ cup strong coffee
- 3 eggs, separated
- Pinch of salt
- 1 tablespoon superfine sugar
- 1 cup cream

COOKING INSTRUCTIONS

1. Add dark chocolate, butter and coffee into a small saucepan over low heat and melt until the mixture is smooth.

2. Stir in egg yolks with salt and mix well.

3. Leave aside.

4. Stiffly beat egg whites using an electric beater on high and gradually add sugar until soft peaks are formed.

5. Combine a small quantity of egg whites with the chocolate mixture and pour it onto the egg whites.

6. Add cream and gently mix to combine evenly.

7. Divide mousse into 6 individual serving bowls and refrigerate overnight.

MOCHA MOUSSE

INGREDIENTS

7 ounces dark chocolate

4 ounces strong instant coffee

4 eggs

2 tablespoons superfine sugar

COOKING INSTRUCTIONS

1. Double boil or microwave chocolate with coffee.

2. Add egg yolks one by one and beat well.

3. Beat egg whites separately until soft peaks form. Gradually add sugar until the peaks begin to harden and make sure not to over beat.

4. Add egg whites in three portions and mix well.

5. Soon as the mousse is evenly mixed, pour into a serving bowl and refrigerate for an hour.

DARK CHOCOLATE MOUSSE WITH CACAO NIBS

INGREDIENTS

- 2 cups whole milk
- ⅔ cup sugar
- 5 extra large egg yolks
- 16 ounces semi-sweet dark chocolate
- 4 cups heavy whipping cream
- 3 tablespoons cacao nibs
- 1 tablespoon coarse sea salt (optional)

COOKING INSTRUCTIONS

1. Chop the chocolate.
2. Melt chocolate on a double boiler.
3. Boil milk and leave aside.
4. Beat egg yolks and sugar separately in a mixing bowl.
5. Stir in a little hot milk to the egg mixture and mix well.
6. Pour the egg mixture in the milk pan.
7. Mix well and cook over a low flame, stirring continuously until the mixture thickens.
8. Pour a tablespoon of hot milk and egg mixture and blend with the chocolate mixture.

9. Pour the entire mixture into the chocolate and mix well.

10. Cool at room temperature.

11. Whip cream on medium using an electric or hand mixer until a soft peaks form.

12. Gently combine with the chocolate mixture and pour the mousse into a bowl. Refrigerate for a minimum of an hour.

13. Garnish with chopped cacao nibs and sea salt to taste. Serve.

EASY, RICH CHOCOLATE MOUSSE (SUGAR-FREE)

INGREDIENTS

¼ cup brewed coffee

¼ cup half and half

1 ½ teaspoons vanilla extract

3 ½ ounces unsweetened chocolate

Artificial sweetener or honey to taste

2 eggs, preferably organic, room temperature

2 ounces cream cheese

COOKING INSTRUCTIONS

1. Microwave coffee with half and half for 50 seconds or until it starts boiling.

2. Chip unsweetened chocolates.

3. Blend together coffee mixture, sweeteners, chopped chocolate and vanilla in a blender until chocolate is melted.

4. Stir in eggs with cream cheese and blend.

5. Check for your preferred sweetness and add more if you prefer.

6. Distribute evenly into serving glasses and refrigerate 3 to 4 hours or until set.

7. Top with sugar-free sweetened heavy cream and garnish with chocolate, a few mint leaves and raspberries.

8. For dairy free and paleo diet, substitute half and half with coconut milk and substitute cream cheese with coconut oil.

CHOCOLATE MOUSSE WITH SALTED CARAMEL ICE CREAM

INGREDIENTS

For the Chocolate Mousse:

6 ounces Semi-sweet or dark chocolate

2 egg yolks

¼ cup sugar

2 tablespoons espresso coffee

1 ½ cups heavy cream

Salted caramel ice cream

Toasted hazelnuts (filberts)

COOKING INSTRUCTIONS

1. Melt chocolate in a double boiler or microwave on low.

2. Beat egg yolks with sugar using a hand beater in a large mixing bowl until the color turns pale.

3. Stir in espresso coffee and melted chocolate.

4. Whip heavy cream until soft peaks form in a medium bowl. Add ⅓ of whip cream and the chocolate mixture.

5. Add the remaining ⅔ of cream in two parts and beat continuously until evenly combined.

6. Distribute mousse evenly into individual dessert bowls and chill for an hour.

Salted Caramel Ice Cream:

1 ¼ cups sugar, divided

2 ¼ cups heavy cream, divided

½ teaspoon flaky sea salt

½ teaspoon pure vanilla extract

1 cup whole milk

3 large eggs

COOKING INSTRUCTIONS

1. In a heavy bottomed saucepan, caramelize a cup of sugar stirring with a fork until the sugar melts and the color turns dark amber.

2. Swirl skillet occasionally, which will help sugar melt evenly.

3. Pour 1 ¼ cups cream and stir until caramel has dissolved.

4. Pour the mixture into a mixing bowl and sprinkle some sea salt and vanilla.

5. Cool completely.

6. Boil milk with the rest of cream. Add ¼ cup sugar, stirring continuously in a heavy bottomed sauce pan.

7. In a medium bowl, slightly beat egg whites and gently stir in half of the hot mixture, stirring continuously.

8. Transfer the contents back to a saucepan and cook over a medium flame, stirring continuously until the custard is thick and coats a spoon.

9. An instant read thermometer inserted should indicate 170 degrees F.

10. Distribute custard into a large dessert bowl through a mesh sieve and blend in cooled caramel.

11. Chill custard 3 to 6 hours.

12. Freeze the custard in ice cream maker, following instructions in the manual, and transfer to a container and re-freeze until firm.

CHOCOLATE RASPBERRY PARFAITS WITH GRAHAM CRACKER CRUNCH

INGREDIENTS

1 cup whipping cream

1 cup fresh raspberries

Pudding:

⅓ cup unsweetened Dutch-processed cocoa powder

¼ cup sugar

3 tablespoons cornstarch

Pinch of sea salt

2 cups milk

1 teaspoon pure vanilla extract

Graham Cracker Crunch:

4 graham crackers, about 1 ounce total

2 tablespoons dark brown sugar

2 tablespoons unsalted butter, cut into small chunks

1 teaspoon pure vanilla extract

Pinch of cinnamon

Pinch of salt

COOKING INSTRUCTIONS

1. Add cocoa powder, sugar, cornstarch and a pinch of salt into a medium sauce pan and pour milk, stirring continuously over a medium flame until the dry ingredients has dissolved completely and the mixture thickens.

DESSERT RECIPES FOR CHOCOLATE LOVERS!

2. Turn off flame and stir in vanilla.

3. Pour the pudding into a large bowl and cover the top surface of pudding with a plastic wrap and refrigerate for 20 minutes until cooled completely.

4. Preheat oven to 350 degrees F.

5. Grease an 8 x 8-inch square pan with butter.

6. Crush the graham crackers and mix with butter, vanilla, cinnamon and salt until smooth and evenly combined.

7. Press it on the bottom of the square pan evenly until the base is firm and bake for 7 to 8 minutes until golden brown on top.

8. Whip cream with vanilla extract and set aside.

9. Place a ¼ spoon of pudding in a serving bowl with ¼ spoon whipped cream and a ¼ raspberry.

10. Crush graham cracker into bite size pieces and sprinkle on top of the raspberry and cream.

ANISEED AND CHOCOLATE PARFAIT

INGREDIENTS

3.75 ounces dark chocolate, chopped

1 ¼ cups heavy cream

1 egg, separated

2 tablespoons superfine sugar

4 ounces mascarpone

8 aniseed cake biscuits, chopped

⅓ cup chilled espresso coffee

Cocoa powder, to dust

COOKING INSTRUCTIONS

1. Melt chocolate with ⅓ of cream on a double boiler until the mixture is smooth, stirring continuously.

2. Beat egg whites until soft peaks form using an electric mixer.

3. Beat together egg yolks with sugar in a separate medium bowl until creamy. Mix in mascarpone.

4. Beat the rest of the cream until soft peaks form using an electric mixture.

5. Add the egg yolk and egg whites and mix to combine evenly.

6. Mix biscuits with coffee and distribute evenly onto the bottom of serving glasses and fill with half chocolate sauce and half cream mixture.

7. Continue layering once or twice with chocolate sauce and cream mixture.

8. Sprinkle with cocoa on top and serve.

CHOCOLATE AVOCADO FUDGE

INGREDIENTS

1 pound bittersweet (or semi-sweet) chocolate, chopped

2 ounces ripe avocado, pureed

1 (14-ounce) can sweetened condensed milk

1 teaspoon vanilla extract

¾ teaspoon salt

COOKING INSTRUCTIONS

1. Grease with butter and line with parchment paper an 8 inch baking pan.

2. In a medium bowl add all ingredients and double boil, stirring continuously until the chocolate is melted and the mixture is smooth.

3. Spread the mixture into the baking pan and refrigerate for 2 hours until firm.

4. Dip a knife or spatula in hot water and wipe.

5. Run the warm knife around the fudge and unmold.

6. Cut into 1 inch squares and store in an airtight container and refrigerate.

SUNDAE COOKIE BARS

INGREDIENTS

1 cup butter, softened
½ cup granulated sugar
¾ cup packed light brown sugar
1 teaspoon vanilla extract
2 eggs
2 ¼ cups all-purpose flour
1 teaspoon baking soda
½ teaspoon salt
2 cups semi-sweet chocolate chips
¼ to ½ cup hot fudge ice cream topping, softened
¼ cup to ½ cup caramel ice cream topping, softened

COOKING INSTRUCTIONS

1. Preheat oven to 350 degrees F.

2. Line with parchment or cooking spray a 9 x 13-inch baking dish.

3. Beat butter and sugar until creamy.

4. Add vanilla and eggs one at a time and beat until evenly incorporated.

5. Mix together flour, baking soda and salt in a separate bowl and stir in to the butter mixture, beating well until evenly combined.

6. Add chocolate chips and stir.

7. Press the dough in the baking dish to a thin layer.

8. Pour a thin layer of hot fudge sauce on top, covering the dough completely.

9. Pour a thin layer of caramel sauce over the fudge sauce.

10. Cover the top of the caramel sauce with the remaining dough.

11. Bake for 25 to 35 minutes.

TRUFFLE-STUFFED CHOCOLATE CHIP COOKIES

INGREDIENTS

For the Truffles:

5 ounces finely chopped semi-sweet or bittersweet chocolate

4 ounces heavy cream

1 tablespoon butter, softened to room temperature

For the Cookies:

2 ¼ cups all-purpose flour

½ teaspoon baking soda

½ teaspoon salt

6 ounces butter, melted, not hot

1 packed cup brown sugar

½ cup granulated sugar

1 egg, room temperature

1 egg yolk, room temperature

1 tablespoon vanilla extract

1 ⅓ cups chocolate chips

COOKING INSTRUCTIONS

To Make the Truffles:

1. Add chopped chocolate into a bowl.

2. Heat heavy cream in a saucepan over medium heat and pour over the chopped chocolates. Let stand for a few minutes.

3. Beat the cream until chocolate is melted and stir in room temperature butter. Mix until the ganache is evenly incorporated.

4. Cover the top of ganache with plastic wrap and refrigerate for 60 to 90 minutes until firm.

5. Scoop 20 small balls from the ganache using a candy scoop or a teaspoon.

6. Dust palm with cocoa powder and roll them into evenly round balls.

7. Refrigerate until firm. Keeps well in an airtight container for 2 weeks.

TO MAKE THE COOKIES:

1. Preheat oven to 325 degrees F.

2. Sift together flour, baking soda and salt.

3. Cream together butter and sugar in a stand mixer on medium speed until the sugar is incorporated.

4. Add eggs and beat until evenly mixed together.

5. Add egg yolk with vanilla; beat well.

6. Stir in flour mixture and mix well until evenly combined.

7. Add chocolate chips and mix to evenly distribute.

8. The dough can be refrigerated until use.

9. Make 1.5 inch balls from the cookie dough and press center to flatten.

10. Place a truffle in the center and cover with another flat dough quarter the size of the bottom cookie and pinch bottom and top.

11. Roll to form a ball.

12. Repeat with entire dough.

13. Place on baking parchment.

14. Bake for 12 to 13 minutes, rotating halfway through until the color has changed and dough has spread.

Cool on the tray for a while and move to a serving plate using a spatula.

These cookies taste best while warm; reheat in microwave for 10 to 15 seconds, if very cold.

S'MORES CHOCOLATE BARS

INGREDIENTS
½ pound milk chocolate
1 jar marshmallow fluff
Dozen graham crackers

Special Tools:
Chocolate bar mold
Kitchen torch (optional)

COOKING INSTRUCTIONS

1. Temper chocolate in the microwave by regulating its temperature.

2. To make custom candies fill molds with ¾ of tempered chocolate and add any dried fruits, nuts, confections, cookies or cereals. Leave to set.

3. For a simplified candy bar, add mini-marshmallows or graham crackers.

TO MAKE THE S'MORES CANDY BAR:

1. Pour tempered chocolate into molds and turn it over a plate and tap the mold with the back of a knife or spatula, removing excess chocolate. Leave to set.

2. The chocolate should coat the mold to resemble a mold.

3. Add marshmallow cream in a bowl.

4. Toast the surface until the marshmallow cream gets a toasted flavor and stirring occasionally; cool completely.

5. Spread a layer of cream on the chocolate mold and place a single layer of graham crackers.

6. Spread a thin layer of chocolate on top. Cover the entire candy bar evenly and let it set until firm.

ESPRESSO TRUFFLE BROWNIES WITH ESPRESSO CHOCOLATE GANACHE AND WHIPPED CREAM

INGREDIENTS

1 cup unsalted butter, extra for greasing tin

1 tablespoon Dutch-process cocoa, extra for dusting tin

12 ounces good quality semi-sweet chocolate, finely chopped

¼ cup freshly brewed espresso

1 tablespoon pure vanilla extract

1 ¼ cups light brown sugar

4 large eggs

½ cup all-purpose flour

¼ teaspoon salt

½ cup walnuts, toasted, cooled and finely ground

1 cup good quality bittersweet or semi-sweet chocolate

COOKING INSTRUCTIONS

1. Preheat oven to 350 degrees F.

2. Grease a 2 x 8-inch square baking dish with butter and line with baking parchment.

3. Lightly dust some cocoa.

4. Melt chocolate in a double boiler under a low flame.

5. Blend together hot espresso, cocoa and vanilla until the ingredients are evenly dissolved.

6. Pour the espresso mixture into the chocolate and mix.

7. Stir in sugar and blend.

8. Add eggs one at a time beating after each addition until well combined to a smooth batter.

9. Sift together flour and salt and stir in to the chocolate mixture and mix until evenly incorporated.

10. Add ground nuts and stir.

11. Stir in chocolate chips, if preferred.

DARK CHOCOLATE CUPCAKES WITH CHOCOLATE MASCARPONE BUTTER CREAM

INGREDIENTS

For the Cupcakes:

2 cups sugar

1¾ cups all-purpose flour

¾ cup Hershey's "Special Dark" Cocoa

1½ teaspoons baking powder

1½ teaspoons baking soda

1 teaspoon salt

2 eggs

1 cup milk

½ cup canola oil

2 teaspoons vanilla extract

1 cup boiling water or 1 cup hot brewed coffee

For the Mascarpone Buttercream:

4 ouncces (½ of an 8 ounce tub) mascarpone cheese

½ cup butter, softened

⅓ cup Hershey's "Special Dark" Cocoa

2 tablespoons milk

2 teaspoons vanilla

1 16 ounce box powdered sugar, sifted

COOKING INSTRUCTIONS

Make the Cupcakes:

1. Preheat oven to 350 degrees F.

2. Line a muffin tray with paper cups.

3. In a large bowl sift together flour, baking powder, baking soda and add salt with sugar and stir.

4. Beat in eggs, milk, oil and vanilla.

5. Beat on high speed using a hand mixer.

6. Pour boiling water or coffee and mix well.

7. Fill muffin pan with ⅔ of batter each and bake for 22 to 25 minutes.

8. Cool completely on a wire rack.

MAKE THE MASCARPONE BUTTERCREAM:

1. Add mascarpone cheese, butter, cocoa powder, milk and vanilla into a large mixing bowl and beat on high speed until the mixture is evenly incorporated.

2. Stir in powdered sugar and beat well to smooth mixture.

3. Stir in extra milk if necessary to acquire the consistency for cupcakes.

CHOCOLATE TOFU MOUSSE

INGREDIENTS

5 ounces soft silken tofu

7 ounces dark or milk chocolate, broken into pieces

1 tablespoon maple syrup

½ teaspoon vanilla extract

COOKING INSTRUCTIONS

1. Process tofu using a hand blender until smooth.

2. Melt chocolate in a double boiler, stirring continuously until the chocolate is melted.

3. Add tofu, chocolate syrup and vanilla into the melted chocolate and mix well.

4. Distribute evenly into 4 small serving bowls and refrigerate for 2 hours.

CHOCOLATE TRES LECHES CAKE

INGREDIENTS

For the Cake:

1½ cups gluten-free all-purpose flour

1 cup Dutch cocoa, sifted

½ teaspoon baking soda

2 ½ teaspoons baking powder

1 ½ teaspoons xanthan gum

½ teaspoon table salt

¾ cup unsalted butter, room temperature

¾ cup dark brown sugar

1 cup granulated sugar

3 large eggs

2 egg yolks

2 teaspoons vanilla

1½ cups buttermilk

COOKING INSTRUCTIONS

1. Preheat oven to 350 degrees F.

2. Grease a 9 x 13-inch baking pan with butter.

3. In a medium bowl sift together gluten-free all purpose flour, cocoa, xanthan gum, baking powder, baking soda and salt

4. Beat butter in a separate bowl until creamy using a stand mixer.

5. Stir in brown sugar and granulated sugar.

6. Beat until light and fluffy.

7. Stir in egg yolks one at a time and beat.

8. Add vanilla and turn the mixer to low.

9. Gradually add the flour mixture with buttermilk and continue beating until the batter is evenly incorporated.

10. Pour into the baking pan and bake for 30 to 35 minutes.

11. Cool completely.

For the Glaze:
1 (12-ounce) can evaporated milk
1 (14-ounce) can sweetened condensed milk
1 cup half-and-half

COOKING INSTRUCTIONS

Add all three ingredients into a mixing bowl and whisk until incorporated and pour the glaze over cake and refrigerate overnight.

For the Topping:
2 cups heavy cream
8 ounces sugar
1 teaspoon vanilla extract
Maraschino cherries, for garnish

COOKING INSTRUCTIONS

1. Beat together heavy cream, sugar and vanilla using a stand mixer until soft peaks form on low speed, and then turn to medium and continue beating until thick.

2. Spread over cake and refrigerate until ready to serve.

CHOCOLATE SOUFFLÉ

INGREDIENTS

Vanilla Pastry Cream Base:

2 cups milk

1½ ounces butter

2 vanilla beans (spilt and scraped)

1½ ounces corn starch

4 egg yolks

Chocolate Soufflé:

3½ egg whites

1½ ounces sugar

Pinch of salt

1½ ounces vanilla pastry cream base

3.75 ounces chocolate

Butter 4 ramekins and coat with sugar

COOKING INSTRUCTIONS

1. Preheat oven to 425 degrees F.

2. Add half the milk, entire butter and 2 vanilla beans into a saucepan.

3. Heat over a medium flame.

4. Pour the other half of milk into a bowl and beat with cornstarch and egg yolks to make slurry.

5. Stir in the slurry to the milk as it starts scalding and mix together and boil.

6. Remove from heat and leave aside.

7. Double boil and melt chocolate.

8. Beat eggs until frothy using a stand mixer on medium speed and increase one more speed and continue beating until stiff.

9. Combine 1½ ounces pastry cream with melted chocolate for the base.

10. Stir in meringue in three portions with the chocolate mixture and mix well.

11. Flatten the mixture using a spatula into ramekins and wipe rim with your thumb and bake for 11 to 12 minutes.

TIRAMISU ICE CREAM CAKE

INGREDIENTS

1 Vanilla sponge cake, baked in a 9-inch square pan (see below)

2 pints chocolate ice cream, softened (leave container at room temperature for about 10 minutes)

2 pints coffee ice cream (leave container at room temperature for about 10 minutes)

2 cups Mascarpone Cream (see below)

About 1 tablespoon cocoa powder

Chocolate curls (made from 6 to 8 ounces of chocolate)

COOKING INSTRUCTIONS

1. Leave ice cream out for 10 minutes at room temperature to soften.

2. Slice sponge into two layers horizontally and place a layer on a flat tray lined with parchments.

3. Line a 9-inch square cake pan with baking parchment with excess parchment sticking out, which will help to unmold. Spread softened ice cream evenly and freeze until firm.

4. Soften coffee ice cream.

5. Unmold the ice cream that's set in the freezer over the sponge layer and press ice cream gently into the sponge

so that the sponge and ice cream stick together and freeze.

6. Line another cake pan with parchment as you did for the ice cream and spread coffee ice cream evenly and freeze until firm.

7. Once set, take both ice creams and place the second sponge layer over the chocolate ice cream and unmold coffee ice cream over the second sponge layer and press gently and freeze for 15 minutes until set.

8. Prepare mascarpone cream.

9. Transfer cake into a serving plate using two spatulas and spread mascarpone cream and garnish with cocoa powder and chocolate curls on top.

10. Keep frozen until required.

For Sponge Cake:
Softened butter, for pan
½ cup all-purpose flour, plus more for pan
½ cup cornstarch
4 large eggs, separated
1 teaspoon pure vanilla extract
¾ cup sugar
Pinch of salt

COOKING INSTRUCTIONS FOR SPONGE CAKE

1. Preheat oven to 350 degrees F.

2. Grease a 9-inch square pan with butter and dust with flour.

3. Sift together flour and cornstarch.

4. Beat egg yolks with vanilla and ½ cup sugar using an electric mixer on high speed until evenly combined.

5. Beat egg whites until stiff peaks form using a clean hand mixer and bowl; separately, on low speed, gradually add ¼ cup of sugar.

6. Mix egg whites with egg yolk in three portions and gradually stir in flour mixture.

7. Spread on cake pans and bake for 40 minutes checking after 35 minutes.

8. Cool completely for 15 minutes and transfer to a wire rack.

For Mascarpone Cream:
½ cup mascarpone cheese
1 cup heavy whipping cream
Optional: 2 to 4 tablespoons sugar

COOKING INSTRUCTIONS FOR MASCARPONE CREAM

1. Beat mascarpone cheese for 60 seconds until creamy.

2. Whip cream in a separate bowl until soft peaks form, gradually adding sugar, if you prefer.

3. Combine whipped cream with cream cheese and mix well.

4. Refrigerate until used.

CHOCOLATE BLITZEN

INGREDIENTS

2 ounces semi-sweet chocolate

⅓ cup chocolate-flavored sprinkles

1 cup chocolate ice cream

2 ounces Irish cream liqueur

1 ounces dark cream de cacao

1 ounce vodka

Chocolate curls or grated chocolate

COOKING INSTRUCTIONS

1. Melt chocolate over a low flame.

2. Dip 8 rims of 1-ounce mini-martini glasses or shot glasses in melted chocolate and sprinkles and chill.

3. Blend ice cream, Irish liqueur, cream de cacao and vodka until the mixture is smooth.

4. Divide into serving glasses and garnish with chocolate curls and serve.

ESPRESSO CHOCOLATE GANACHE

INGREDIENTS

1 cup heavy whipping cream

4 teaspoons instant espresso powder

1 tablespoon golden corn syrup

10 ounces good quality bittersweet or semi-sweet chocolate, finely chopped

COOKING INSTRUCTIONS

1. Add chocolate into a heat proof bowl.

2. Add cream and espresso in a saucepan and heat over medium flame until espresso has melted and bubbles form.

3. Turn off heat and keep covered for 30 minutes.

4. Strain the coffee and add corn syrup.

5. Simmer over a medium flame until bubbles start forming on the sides of the pan and the corn syrup dissolves, stirring continuously.

6. Stir the mixture of chocolate; leave aside for 2 minutes.

7. Mix chocolate until it melts and the mixture is smooth using a spatula.

8. Pour over cooled brownies and leave at room temperature for 3 hours for the ganache to set.

WHIPPED CREAM TOPPING

INGREDIENTS

1 cup heavy cream

2 tablespoons powdered sugar, sifted

½ teaspoon vanilla extract

COOKING INSTRUCTIONS

1. Chill a large bowl, beater and cream.

2. Add cream, powdered sugar and vanilla into the bowl and beat using a hand mixer until soft peaks form

3. Chill until required.

TO SERVE ESPRESSO TRUFFLE BROWNIES:

Sweetened whipped cream, optional

Chocolate covered espresso beans, optional

1. Unmold brownie from tray and cut squares using a spatula dipped in hot water and wiped.

2. Fill whipped cream in a pastry bag with a plain tip and pipe per each piece of brownie and top it with an espresso bean.

PUDDING

FIG AND CHOCOLATE PUDDING WITH CARAMEL SAUCE

INGREDIENTS

- 1 cup butter
- 17 ½ ounces fig jam
- ½ cup brown sugar
- 2 eggs
- ¼ cup cocoa
- 1 ½ cups self-rising flour
- ¾ cup milk (6 ounces)

COOKING INSTRUCTIONS

1. Preheat oven to 355 degrees F

2. Blend together butter, sugar and jam until soft.

3. Beat in eggs with the butter mixture.

4. Sift cocoa with flour and add ⅓ to the egg mixture with ⅓ milk.

5. Add the remaining flour and milk in two portions and mix well.

6. Pour the mixture into a baking dish or 6 small ramekins and bake for 45 minutes until done. Check early.

7. Cool and serve with caramel.

Caramel Sauce:
1½ ounces butter
1 cup brown sugar
½ cup cream

COOKING INSTRUCTIONS

1. Add all three ingredients into a saucepan and boil over a low flame.

2. Slightly cool and serve.

DARK AND WHITE CHOCOLATE PUDDING WITH MARSHMALLOWS

INGREDIENTS

5.25 ounces dark chocolate chips

4 ounces white chocolate chips plus extra 1 ounce to add to the pudding (not melted) and some more to decorate

7 ounces chocolate flavored marshmallows

2 ounces butter at room temperature

2 ½ ounces tablespoons of water

1 teaspoon pure vanilla extracts

1 ¼ cups cream

COOKING INSTRUCTIONS

1. Add dark chocolate, white chocolate chips, marshmallows and butter into a saucepan and double boil over medium heat, stirring continuously until the chocolate is melted with the butter and marshmallows are slightly melted, but still in shape.

2. Turn off heat and stir in vanilla extract.

3. Whip cream until stiff peaks form and combine with the chocolate mixture with an extra 1 ounce of white chocolate chips.

4. Distribute evenly into 6 to 8 individual serving bowls and refrigerate 4 to 5 hours.

5. Garnish with some white chocolate chips and serve chilled.

BOOZY CHOCOLATE PUDDING

INGREDIENTS

¼ ounce gelatin

4 tablespoons cold water

1 cup whole milk

1 cup heavy cream

½ cup sugar, divided

6 egg yolks

5 ounces dark chocolate, chopped

1 teaspoon pure vanilla extract

¼ cup Amaretto

COOKING INSTRUCTIONS

1. Add water with gelatin in a small ramekin, mix and leave aside.

2. Pour milk, cream and add ¼ cup sugar in a 2 quart-size sauce pan and beat altogether.

3. Heat the mixture, stirring continuously on a medium flame; leave aside.

4. Add ¼ cup sugar and egg yolks into a mixing bowl and beat at medium to high speed until the color becomes light and the mixture is creamy.

5. Gently combine the egg mixture with the milk mixture and beat.

6. Over a medium flame simmer the mixture with chocolate and cook, stirring continuously until the chocolate melts.

7. Take the mixture off heat and beat, adding vanilla, Amaretto and gelatin. Continue cooking until the mixture thickens.

8. Pour the pudding evenly in desired bowls and refrigerate for at least 2 hours until set.

SPICED CHOCOLATE PUDDING

INGREDIENTS

3 cups coconut milk, divided
¼ cup cornstarch
⅓ cup sugar
1 tablespoon. cinnamon
A pinch of cayenne pepper, optional
1 cup vegan chocolate chips
Pinch salt
1 teaspoon pure vanilla extract

COOKING INSTRUCTIONS

1. Combine a cup of coconut milk and cornstarch in a heavy bottom pan.

2. Beat until the mixture is creamy with no lumps.

3. Pour in the other 2 cups of coconut milk, sugar, cinnamon, salt and cayenne.

4. Cook the mixture over medium high heat, stirring continuously until it reaches a boiling stage.

5. Reduce heat and continue cooking.

6. Stir in chocolate chips and beat until the chocolate melts.

7. Take off heat and add vanilla and cool for a few minutes.

8. Pour the pudding into a pudding bowl and spread a piece of plastic wrap and make sure it touches the top of the pudding, which will prevent it from forming a top layer.

9. Serve with a scoop of ice cream, if preferred.

TOFU CHOCOLATE PUDDING

INGREDIENTS

¾ cup semisweet chocolate chips

1 tablespoon water

12 ounces packet silken tofu

COOKING INSTRUCTIONS

1. Drain the tofu to remove excess moisture.

2. Double boil chocolate chips with some water until 80% is melted and remove from double boiler. Continue beating until the remaining chocolate chips are melted; leave aside.

3. Blend tofu until smooth.

4. Beat ingredients together until smooth.

5. Cool for 2 hours or more in the refrigerator.

6. Spread into serving bowls and garnish with nuts and cherries; dust with some chocolate.

BAKED HONEY CHOCOLATE PUDDING

INGREDIENTS

Greek Yogurt:

7.50 ounces dark chocolate, 75% cocoa solids

7.50 ounces butter, diced

4 ounces golden caster sugar

4 egg yolks

4 large eggs

2 ounces plain flour, sifted

COOKING INSTRUCTIONS

1. Preheat oven at 350 degrees F.

2. Grease eight ramekin dishes with butter. Dust some flour and line with baking parchment paper at the bottom.

3. Beat together sugar, egg yolk and eggs until stiff peaks form.

4. Gently combine chocolate mixture with egg mixture and stir in flour and mix together.

5. Pour the mixture into the prepared ramekins and bake for 7 minutes or until the puddings are risen and cooked evenly.

6. Leave to cool in a warm place.

7. Turn the pudding onto a flat plate and serve with a spoonful of Greek yogurt and some honey on top.

VEGAN CHOCOLATE PUMPKIN PUDDING

INGREDIENTS

1 banana, peeled

4 ounces pure pumpkin puree

¼ cup cocoa powder

2 packs of whey protein powder

1 teaspoon cinnamon

½ teaspoon vanilla extracts

½ cup almond milk

COOKING INSTRUCTIONS

1. Blend together banana, pumpkin purée, cocoa powder, whey protein powder, cinnamon and vanilla extract in a food processor.

2. Add almond milk to the food processor, scrape sides and blend well until combined equally.

3. Refrigerate for an hour.

4. Serve cool.

DESSERT RECIPES FOR CHOCOLATE LOVERS!

COOKIES

TRIPLE CHOCOLATE FUDGE COOKIES

INGREDIENTS

8 ounces unsalted butter
5 ounces superfine sugar
6 ounces brown sugar
1 teaspoon vanilla extract
1 egg
9.5 ounces plain flour, sifted
0.75 ounces cocoa, sifted
1 teaspoon bicarbonate of soda
1 ounce chopped roasted hazelnuts
Pinch of salt
8 ounces dark chocolate, chopped
5 ounces white chocolate, chopped

COOKING INSTRUCTIONS

1. Preheat the oven to 356 degrees F. Line a baking sheet with parchment paper.

2. In the bowl of an electric mixer add the butter, caster sugar, brown sugar and vanilla extract. Beat until it becomes thick and pale. Add in the egg and mix well. Sift the flour, cocoa and baking soda. Stir in the hazelnuts, 7 ounces of the dark chocolate and 4 ounces of the white chocolate. Roll the dough into small balls. You can freeze any amount of the balls at this stage, if you don't want to bake all 36 cookies at this time. Arrange the balls on the baking sheet about 5 cm apart leaving enough room for expansion. If you are making all of the cookies do them in batches. Slightly press down on each ball with your hand. Bake the batch for 12 minutes or until the cookies are just dry on the surface. Cool the cookies on the baking sheet until somewhat firm. This should take about 5 minutes. Transfer the cookies onto a wire rack to cool completely.

3. Melt the remaining 1 ounce of dark chocolate while stirring in a double boiler. Drizzle the chocolate over the cookies. Repeat the process with the 1 ounce of white chocolate. Continue cooling until the chocolate hardens.

To store the dough, put the cookie balls on a baking sheet and put them in the freezer until frozen. Take them out of the freezer and place them in a freezer bag. Store the bag in the freezer until you are ready to bake. Then take out as many cookies as you want to bake and place them on a baking paper lined baking sheet. Preheat oven to 356 degrees F and leave them in the oven for 15 to18 minutes, heating from frozen.

CHOCOLATE AND RED WINE COOKIES

INGREDIENTS

1 stick unsalted butter

¾ cup brown sugar

¾ cup sugar

1 egg

1 teaspoon vanilla

½ cup red wine*

1½ cups flour

¾ cup unsweetened Dutch cocoa powder

1 teaspoon salt

1 teaspoon baking soda

½ cup semi-sweet chocolate chips (mine happened to be mini)

*I use a mulled wine, "Glögg"–a perfect match for chocolate. Glögg is a red wine containing various spices and raisins.

COOKING INSTRUCTIONS

1. Preheat the oven to 375 degrees F. Line two baking sheets with parchment paper or use a nonstick baking mat.

2. Cream the butter and sugars until light and fluffy. Stir in the egg, vanilla, and red wine. If you like, sample the red wine first!

3. Combine the flour, salt, cocoa powder, and baking soda in a small bowl. Sift the dry ingredients into the wet mixture. Stir the dough until you just combine the ingredients. Finally, add in the chocolate chips.

4. Measure out small spoonfuls of the dough onto the baking sheets. I use 1 tablespoon to make small cookies. Allow for some room for the cookies to spread.

5. Bake for 8 minutes, then remove from the oven. Cool on the cookie sheets for a few minutes.

NUTELLA STUFFED BROWN BUTTER AND SEA SALT CHOCOLATE CHIP COOKIES

INGREDIENTS

2 ¼ cups all-purpose flour

1 ¼ teaspoons baking soda

¼ teaspoon of salt

2 sticks (1 cup) unsalted butter

1 ¼ cups packed dark brown sugar

¼ cup granulated sugar

1 large egg plus 1 egg yolk

1 ½ teaspoons vanilla extract

1 tablespoon plain Greek yogurt

¾ cup semi-sweet chocolate chips

½ cup milk chocolate chips

½ cup dark chocolate chips

1 jar of Nutella, chilled in refrigerator

Coarse sea salt for sprinkling

COOKING INSTRUCTIONS

1. Sift the flour, baking soda, and salt in a bowl and set aside. Melt butter in a saucepan over medium heat until it begins to foam. Whisk the butter continually for a few minutes until the butter begins to brown on the bottom of the saucepan and has a nutty fragrance. Put the melted butter in a bowl to prevent burning. Set aside to cool for a few minutes.

2. Mix the butter and sugars until completely blended with an electric mixer. Mix in the egg, yolk, vanilla, and yogurt until combined. Slowly stir in the dry ingredients. Change the setting to low on the mixer and beat until combined. Gently fold in all of the chocolate chips.

3. The dough should chill in the refrigerator for 2 hours or in the freezer for 30 minutes. The recommended method is chilling in the refrigerator.

4. Preheat the oven to 350 degrees F. After the chilling the dough, roll 1½ tablespoons of dough into a ball. Use the palm of your hand to flatten the dough until it is thin. In the center of the cookie add 1 teaspoon of chilled Nutella. Fold the dough around the Nuttela. Gently roll the dough into a ball. It does not need to be perfect. Be sure that the Nutella is not running out of the dough. Use more dough if needed. Put the balls on a cookie sheet 2 inches apart. Use the palm of your hand to VERY gently flatten the balls only on the tops.

5. Bake until the edge of the cookies turn golden brown. This should take about 9 to 11 minutes. They will be soft in the middle, but the cookies will continue to cook once they are out of the oven. The cookies should cool on the baking sheets for about 2 minutes. Sprinkle them with a little sea salt and put them on a wire rack to cool fully. Repeat this process with the leftover dough.

PEANUT BUTTER OATMEAL WHITE CHOCOLATE COOKIES

INGREDIENTS

½ cup butter

⅓ cup peanut butter

1 cup brown sugar

½ cup white sugar

1 egg + 1 yolk

2 teaspoons vanilla extract

1¼ cups all-purpose flour

1 cup old fashioned whole oats

½ teaspoon baking soda

¾ cup white chocolate chips

½ cup peanut butter chips (or use butterscotch chips, chocolate chips, toffee bits, raisins, nuts, seeds, etc.)

COOKING INSTRUCTIONS

1. Melt the butter and peanut butter together in the microwave. Heat the mixture for 30 seconds. Remove it from the microwave and stir. Repeat. It should not take more than 90 seconds to mix the butter and peanut butter together in the microwave.

2. Stir in the brown and white sugars to the melted butter and peanut butter mixture. Put this combination in the freezer for a few minutes.

3. Remove the bowl from the freezer and add the egg plus yolk once it has cooled to room temperature. It is important not to add the egg and yolk in if the mix is too hot. Stir in the vanilla extract.

4. Stir in the flour, oats and baking soda. The mixture should have the consistency of dough. Add a bit more flour if it is too wet or a bit more peanut butter if it is too dry.

5. Fold in the white chocolate chips and peanut butter chips and stir.

6. Put golf ball sized balls of dough onto a cookie sheet approximately two inches apart. The cookies will spread slightly during baking.

7. Bake at 325 degrees F. for about 10 to 12 minutes. For softer cookies bake for 10 minutes. The cookies will look slightly underdone, but they will continue to cook while they are cooling. Cool the cookies before eating.

For vegan cookies use margarine instead of butter and use vegan white chocolate chips. For the eggs use two flax or chia 'eggs' or other egg replacements.

To make gluten-free use gluten-free flour. Be sure to note the trace of gluten in the other ingredients.

CHOCOLATE COVERED STRAWBERRY COOKIES

INGREDIENTS

1 cup semi-sweet chocolate chips

¾ cup (about 6 ounces) dried strawberries

½ cup granulated sugar

½ cup packed light brown sugar

½ cup unsalted butter, at room temperature

1 large egg

1 teaspoon vanilla extract

½ teaspoon baking soda

1¼ cups all-purpose flour

¼ teaspoon salt

COOKING INSTRUCTIONS

1. It is best to prep the chocolate covered strawberries the night before. Alternately, they can be made as soon as 2 hours before the cookies are prepared. In the microwave, melt 1 cup of semi-sweet chocolate chips for 1 minute on high. Be sure to stir the chocolate until all the chips have melted.

2. On wax paper or a baking sheet lined with parchment paper spread out the dried strawberries. Pour the chocolate over each strawberry. (If some of the chocolate gets on the paper it is okay. The strawberries and chocolate will be chopped and added to the cookies later.) The chocolate-covered strawberries should be put in

the refrigerator for at least 2 hours until the chocolate hardens.

3. Preheat the oven to 300 degrees F. Prepare two baking sheets by lining them with parchment paper.

4. Beat the sugars and butter together with an electric mixer on medium speed until smooth. Add in the egg, vanilla, and baking soda. Use the mixer to beat for another 2 minutes on medium speed.

5. Mix the flour and salt in a large mixing bowl. Add the mixture to the batter. Beat until just incorporated. Chop up the chocolate covered strawberries and then add them to the batter by hand.

6. Measure out the cookie dough into heaping tablespoon balls. On the baking sheets put 8 to 12 balls 2 inches apart.

7. Bake in the oven until golden brown for approximately 18 minutes. Cool the cookies on the baking sheets for 5 minutes. Next, put the cookies on a wire rack to completely cool.

8. The cookies can be stored at room temperature for 3 days in an airtight container.

ROCKY ROAD COOKIES

Makes about 16 cookies

INGREDIENTS

½ cup all-purpose flour

¼ cup unsweetened Dutch-process cocoa powder

¼ teaspoon baking soda

¼ teaspoon salt

½ cup semi-sweet or bittersweet chocolate chips (I used ¼ cup of each)

½ stick (4 tablespoons) unsalted butter

¼ cup sugar

1 large egg

½ teaspoon pure vanilla extract

¼ cup chopped walnuts

¼ cup mini-marshmallows

COOKING INSTRUCTIONS

1. Preheat the oven to 325 degrees F.

2. Sift the flour, cocoa powder, baking soda and salt in a medium sized bowl.

3. In a double boiler melt half of the chocolate chips in the butter.

4. Add sugar, egg, and vanilla to the melted chocolate. Use an electric mixer to combine.

5. Slowly add the dry ingredients with the electric mixer on a low speed until just combined.

6. Fold in the remaining chocolate chips, walnuts and marshmallows.

7. On baking sheets lined with parchment paper place about 1 tablespoon of dough about 2 inches apart, making sure that the marshmallows are not exposed. Also be sure that the marshmallows are inside the dough ball as they will melt in the oven. For a twist, you can add a few marshmallows on top of the cookies just before they are done.

8. Bake until the top of the cookie begins to crack for approximately 12 to 15 minutes. To cool, put the cookies on a wire rack. Great served with milk.

BUCKEYE PEANUT BUTTER CUP COOKIES

INGREDIENTS

Cookies:

1 ½ cups all-purpose flour

½ cup unsweetened cocoa powder

½ teaspoon baking soda

¼ teaspoon salt

½ cup unsalted butter, at room temperature

½ cup granulated sugar (plus more for rolling)

½ cup light brown sugar

¼ cup creamy peanut butter

1 egg

1 teaspoon vanilla extract

Filling:

¾ cup creamy peanut butter

¾ cup powdered sugar

COOKING INSTRUCTIONS

1. Preheat oven to 375 degrees F. Prepare two baking sheets by lining them with parchment paper.

2. Mix the flour, cocoa powder, baking soda and salt in a medium bowl; set aside.

3. Cream the butter, sugars and peanut butter with an electric mixer on medium until light and fluffy. It should take about 3 minutes. Beat in the egg and vanilla

extract until combined. With the mixer on low, add the flour mixture and blend until combined.

4. In a separate medium bowl, mix together the peanut butter and powdered sugar for the filling until smooth.

5. Add some extra granulated sugar in a small bowl. This will be used to roll the cookies.

6. With a heaping tablespoon or a medium cookie scoop measure out the cookie dough and flatten it with your hands. Place the peanut butter filling in the center of the chocolate dough. Use about 1 teaspoon of the filling or a small cookie scoop's worth. The dough should be wrapped around the filling and then pressed in to seal. Take the cookie and roll it into a ball. Then roll the dough ball in the sugar. Put the cookies on the baking sheets about 2 inches apart. The dough balls should be flattened slightly with the palm of your hand.

7. Bake the cookies for 7 to 9 minutes. The cookies should be cooled for 2 minutes on the baking sheet. Place the cookies on a wire rack to cool completely. The cookies should be stored in an airtight container at room temperature.

CHOCOLATE ORANGE SANDWICH COOKIES

INGREDIENTS

Sift together:

2 cups flour

1 ½ cups cocoa

Cream together:

1 ½ cups cold butter

¼ cup sugar

1 teaspoon vanilla extract

Zest of 3 oranges, finely grated

COOKING INSTRUCTIONS

1. **To form the dough:** Add the dry ingredients to the creamed mixture. The dough should chill in the refrigerator for about 1 hour. Roll out the dough to about a quarter-inch thick.

2. Use a 2-inch cookie cutter to make individual cookies. Bake at 350 degrees F for 12to 13 minutes. Use a wire rack to cool completely.

Orange Buttercream Filling:

½ cup butter

2 cups icing sugar (powdered sugar)

1 teaspoon vanilla extract

1 tablespoon minced orange zest

3 or 4 tablespoons milk

COOKING INSTRUCTIONS

1. In a medium bowl, add all the ingredients together. Beat until smooth using only enough milk to bring the frosting to a workable consistency. The cream filling should be stiffer than frosting for a cake.

2. To make a sandwich cookie, spoon a teaspoon or so between two of the shortbread cookies.

DESSERT RECIPES FOR CHOCOLATE LOVERS!

CHOCOLATE-COVERED CHERRY COOKIES

INGREDIENTS

1 stick melted butter

1 cup white sugar

1 egg

¼ teaspoon baking powder

¼ teaspoon baking soda

¼ teaspoon salt

1 teaspoon vanilla

½ cup cocoa

1 ½ cups all-purpose flour

1 small jar maraschino cherries

1 cup chocolate chips

¼ cup sweetened condensed milk

COOKING INSTRUCTIONS

1. Preheat oven to 350 degrees F.

2. Mix the sugar into the melted butter in a large bowl. Cool for a few minutes before mixing in the egg.

3. Add in the baking powder, baking soda, salt, vanilla and cocoa into the bowl. Be sure to mix well after each addition.

4. Add the flour slowly while mixing well to make the cookie dough.

5. On a baking sheet line up small balls of dough. On the top of each ball, make a small indentation flattening the dough into a cookie shape in the process.

6. In each cookie indentation place 1 cherry. The juice from the cherries needs to be saved either by saving the juice from draining or by pulling the cherries from the jar.

7. In a double-boiler with simmering water add the chocolate chips and condensed milk. Cook until the chocolate chips melt. The mix will be very, very thick.

8. Using 1 teaspoon at a time add cherry juice until mixture becomes easy to shape. I needed 5 teaspoons to make my mixture more malleable.

9. On top of each cherry, form a bit of the icing. Make sure the icing does not run down the sides of the cookie.

10. Bake for 10 minutes.

DESSERT RECIPES FOR CHOCOLATE LOVERS!

TARTS

SALTED CHOCOLATE TOFFEE TARTS

INGREDIENTS

1 cup all-purpose flour, sifted

½ cup cocoa, sifted

½ cup icing sugar, sifted

½ cup butter, chopped

3 large egg yolks

1 teaspoon vanilla extract

1 tablespoon iced water

1 cup homemade toffee, also known as dulce de leche - see below

¾ cup dark chocolate, chopped for melting

Sea salt flakes, for sprinkling

COOKING INSTRUCTIONS

1. Blend together flour, cocoa, icing sugar and butter in a food processor until the mixture resembles bread crumbs.

2. Add egg yolks and vanilla and continue beating.

3. Pour ice water and blend until the dough sticks together and turn it onto a lightly floured surface and bring the dough together, flatten and wrap in plastic. Refrigerate for 1 hour.

4. Spray tart pans with nonstick spray and baking paper cases.

5. Roll pastry to ¼ thickness and cut circles using a pastry cutter and place on tart.

6. Trim edges of pans and prick with a fork and refrigerate for an hour.

7. Preheat oven to 350 degrees F.

8. Fill pie weights and bake for 10 minutes.

9. Discard paper weights and bake for further 10 minutes.

10. Cool completely and remove.

11. Evenly spread de leche into pastry cases and refrigerate for 10 minutes.

12. Spread over the tarts and sprinkle with sea salt and refrigerate for 2 hours.

TO MAKE HOMEMADE TOFFEE:

1. Place a can of sweetened condensed milk in a small pot filled with enough water to just cover the can and boil over medium flame.

2. Constantly check for the water level to maintain the exact quantity of water throughout the process, adding more water as it evaporates. There is a possibility of the can exploding if the water boils out of the pot!

3. Reduce heat and cook at a slight simmer: For a soft de leche it might take 3 hours and for a firm one 4 hours.

4. Lift can using tongs and cool on a rack.

PRIMAL CHOCOLATE GANACHE TART

INGREDIENTS

10 ounces walnuts
1 ounce. unsalted butter
1 teaspoon baking soda
¼ teaspoon salt
11 ounces dark chocolate
5.6 ounces double cream

COOKING INSTRUCTIONS

1. Preheat oven to 350 degrees F.

2. Grind walnuts using a food processor.

3. Add cubed butter, salt and baking soda.

4. Continue blending until the mixture is evenly combined.

5. Roll out the mixture equally into six, 4-inch tartlets tins and bake for 15 to 20 minutes until slightly golden brown.

6. Par-melt chopped chocolates in a microwave at 50%.

7. Heat the cream in a pan, do not boil.

8. Pour cream over chocolate and stir until the chocolate is completely melted.

9. Pour ganache into tart shells and refrigerate until set.

10. Remove tart shells from the tart tin and serve with whipped cream and a choice of fruit.

CHOCOLATE MOCHA TART WITH KAHLUA MASCARPONE CREAM

INGREDIENTS

Chocolate Tart Shell:

½ cup butter, softened

½ cup powdered sugar

¾ teaspoon vanilla

2 large egg yolks

1¼ cups flour (gluten-free option, see below)

¼ cup cocoa powder, sifted

Chocolate Cream Layer:

1 ¼ cups whipping cream

1 ¼ cups finely chopped high quality semi-sweet chocolate (about 65%)

2 tablespoons Kahlua or prepared espresso

1 tablespoon rum, optional

Kahlua Mascarpone Cream:

1 cup whipping cream

1 ½ cups mascarpone cheese, at room temperature

3 tablespoons powdered sugar

2 tablespoons Kahlua or prepared espresso

2 tablespoons rum, optional

Garnish:

5 ounces high-quality semi-sweet chocolate, grated, plus chocolate curls

COOKING INSTRUCTIONS

Chocolate Tart Shells:

1. Beat together butter and sugar.

2. Stir in vanilla with the egg yolks and mix.

3. Add flour and cocoa and continue mixing on low.

4. Gather the mixture and form a flat circle, wrap it in plastic and refrigerate for an hour.

5. Preheat oven to 350 degrees F.

6. Roll dough into 11 inch diameter tart pan and press down the edges.

7. Prick the bottom with a folk and bake for 20 minutes until slightly firm.

8. Make sure it's enough, but don't overcook.

9. Cool completely on a wire rack.

Chocolate Cream Layer:

1. Add chocolate in a heat proof bowl.

2. Boil cream in a medium saucepan over medium high heat.

3. Pour over the chocolate and stir until the chocolate is completely melted.

4. Add Kahlua or espresso with rum and mix.

5. Cool completely.

6. Distribute into tart shells and refrigerate for 4 hours or overnight.

Kahlua Mascarpone Cream:

1. Whip cream using a hand mixer or stand mixer until stiff peaks form on medium speed.

2. Cream mascarpone cheese in a separate mixing bowl until smooth and creamy and reduce speed.

3. Stir in sugar, rum and Kahlua and continue beating.

4. Combine half of the whipped team and mix well.

5. Stir in the other half of whipped cream and mix well.

6. Spread mascarpone cream over the layer in the tart shells using a spatula and garnish with grated chocolate and chocolate curls. Keep refrigerated.

DARK CHOCOLATE FUDGE TART

INGREDIENTS

Crust:

1 ½ cups almond meal

6 tablespoons cocoa powder

3 tablespoons pure maple syrup

3 tablespoons unprocessed coconut oil

½ teaspoon sea salt

Filling:

1 ½ cups cocoa powder

1 cup plus 2 tablespoons pure maple syrup

2 tablespoons unprocessed coconut oil

½ teaspoon sea salt

COOKING INSTRUCTIONS

1. Blend together all the ingredients for the crust using a food processor, blender or by hand.

2. Divide and roll out dough into 12 muffin cups.

3. Blend together all the filling ingredients until smooth and divide over the tartlets and refrigerate for 2 hours.

DESSERT RECIPES FOR CHOCOLATE LOVERS!

FUDGE

CHOCOLATE COOKIES N' CREAM FUDGE

INGREDIENTS

1 (14-ounce) can sweetened condensed milk

1 teaspoon vanilla extract

2 ½ cups semi-sweet chocolate chips

3 tablespoons unsalted butter, cut into ½-inch pieces, at room temperature

2 tablespoons cocoa powder

8 chocolate cookies, roughly chopped

COOKING INSTRUCTIONS

1. Prepare an 8 x 8-inch baking pan by lining it with a sheet of aluminum. Set the pan aside.

2. Add the condensed milk, vanilla, chocolate chips, and butter in a medium bowl. The bowl should be made out of glass or stainless steel.

3. Add some chocolate chips into the bowl. Place the bowl over some simmering water in a saucepan. Heat the bowl for 6 to 8 minutes until the chocolate chips have melted and are smooth. The mixture will be thick. Stir in the chopped cookies and cocoa powder. Use a spatula to scrape the fudge out of the bowl and put it into the prepared pan. Smooth the top of the fudge with a spatula. Chill for at least 2 hours until firm.

4. Put the fudge on to the cutting board by lifting it out of the pan by the sides of the aluminum foil. Cut into bite sized pieces. Store the fudge in the refrigerator in an airtight container. It can be frozen for later use.

CHOCOLATE PEANUT BUTTER FUDGE

Yield: 25 squares

INGREDIENTS

1 cup semi-sweet chocolate chips or coarsely chopped chocolate

1 cup peanut butter

½ cup butter, cut into tablespoon

1 cup powdered sugar

1 teaspoon vanilla extract

COOKING INSTRUCTIONS

1. Prepare a 9 x 9-inch square baking pan by lightly greasing the bottom and the sides of the pan. Set aside.

2. Put a glass or metal bowl over a saucepan of water heated to a steady simmer. The bottom of the bowl should not actually touch the water. The bowl will be heated by the steam. Place the chocolate into the bowl. Stir until the chocolate is almost smooth. Stir in the peanut butter until almost smooth. Next, stir in the butter and mix until completely smooth.

3. Remove the bowl from the heat. Using a whisk, stir in the sugar and vanilla until blended well. Add the fudge into the prepared pan. Be sure to scrape out the sides of the bowl. Chill the fudge in the refrigerator. Cut the fudge into 25 even squares. Keep the fudge in the refrigerator for storage.

TRIPLE CHOCOLATE FUDGE

Yield: 15 pieces

INGREDIENTS

7 ounces sugar-free dark chocolate

4 ounces 100% cacao unsweetened chocolate

7 ounces sugar-free milk chocolate

COOKING INSTRUCTIONS

1. Prepare a brownie pan by lining with parchment paper both ways.

2. Add each of the chocolates into their own microwave-safe bowl. Heat each of the bowls at 30-second intervals. Stir the chocolate and return to the microwave to heat for an additional 30 seconds. Repeat this process until the chocolate has melted.

3. **To make the bottom layer:** In the dark chocolate, stir in ½ cup to ¾ cup of condensed milk. Start out by adding ½ cup of the milk at first. Work your way up to ¾ of a cup of milk by adding enough so that the mix resembles paste. Put the mix into the brownie pan with a spatula and spread. Freeze this layer while making the second.

4. **To make the middle layer:** In the unsweetened chocolate, stir in ½ cup to 1 cup of the condensed milk. Start out by adding ½ cup at first. Work your way up to 1

cup of milk. The mix will look a little different than the other mixture. Add in even more condensed milk if the mixture looks too dry. Remove the brownie pan from the freezer and scrape the unsweetened chocolate mix on to the bottom layer with a spatula. Return the brownie pan to the freezer.

5. **To make the top layer:** In the milk chocolate, stir in ¾ cup to 1½ cups of condensed milk to the milk chocolate. For "real fudge" use ¾ cup of milk. For the fudge to look more like mine add in 1½ cups of milk. Scrape the milk chocolate mixture into the brownie pan using a spatula. Freeze the brownie pan again until the top layer is firm. Slice and serve from the pan.

DARK M&M FUDGE

INGREDIENTS

½ cup coconut oil, in liquid form

½ cup honey

½ cup plus 2 tablespoons Hershey's Special Dark Cocoa

2 tablespoons almond butter

½ cup dark chocolate M&M's

COOKING INSTRUCTIONS

1. Using a whisk, mix the coconut oil and honey together.

2. Slowly stir in the cocoa powder with the whisk.

3. Next stir in the almond butter with the whisk.

4. Prepare a loaf pan by covering it with a non-stick foil. Pour the mixture into the loaf pan.

5. On top of the mix, add the M&M's.

6. Place the loaf pan in the freezer for 15 minutes.

7. Remove the pan from the freezer and cut it into squares.

8. The fudge can be stored in the refrigerator until ready to eat.

CHOCOLATE MARSHMALLOWS

Yield: 36 pieces

COOKING INSTRUCTIONS

1. Line an 8 x 8-inch pan with plastic wrap. Grease the plastic wrap lightly.

2. Add the gelatin over the water in a small sauce pan. Let the gelatin expand in the pan. Stir the water and gelatin while adding in the sugar over a low heat.

3. Pour the heated sugar and gelatin mixture into the bowl of an electric mixture. Mix in the corn syrup. Beat the mixture for 10 to 12 minutes until stiff peaks form. Use a spatula to mix in the melted chocolate.

4. Use a greased spatula to pour the fudge into the prepared pan. Refrigerate the pan for about 1 hour until the fudge is well set.

5. Use ½ of the cocoa powder to cover a work area. Roll onto the cocoa powder. Cut the marshmallows into squares using scissors or a pizza cutter. Be sure to cover the marshmallow squares with the rest of the cocoa powder.

6. The fudge can be stored at room temperature for 3 to 4 days in a well-sealed container, that is if they last that long.

DARK CHOCOLATE RUM BALLS

INGREDIENTS

6 tablespoons unsalted butter, cut into pieces
3 ounces Semi-sweet chocolate, finely chopped
2 eggs
¼ cup packed light-brown sugar
1 teaspoon pure vanilla extract
¼ teaspoon salt
¼ cup all-purpose flour
2 tablespoons cocoa powder
¼ cup dark rum
Coarse sugar for rolling

COOKING INSTRUCTIONS

1. Preheat oven to 350 degrees F.

2. Spray an 8 x 8-inch baking sheet with cooking spray.

3. Melt chocolate with butter in a microwave or double boiler until the chocolate melts, stirring continuously; if in a microwave, stir after every 15 seconds.

4. Beat eggs, brown sugar and vanilla.

5. Pour over chocolates mixture and combine flour with cocoa.

6. Pour evenly on the baking dish and bake 10 to 12 minutes and cool slightly.

7. Chop brownies and blend using an electric mixer or hand mixer.

8. Gently pour rum and beat until the mixture sticks together forming a ball shape.

9. Shape small balls and roll over crystal sugar and place on a tray lined with baking parchment.

10. Refrigerate for approximately 2 hours and serve.

DESSERT RECIPES FOR CHOCOLATE LOVERS!

TRUFFLES

CHOCOLATE TRUFFLES

INGREDIENTS

6 ounces bittersweet chocolate

6 ounces semi-sweet chocolate

1 ¼ cups heavy cream

For dipping:

8 ounces semi-sweet chocolate plus 2 ounces more semi-sweet chocolate

Toothpicks

Styrofoam

Cocoa powder

Finely chopped nuts

Shredded coconut

Powdered sugar

White chocolate

COOKING INSTRUCTIONS

Middles:

1. Chop the bittersweet chocolate and the semi-sweet chocolate into small pieces. Place the chocolate in to separate bowls.

2. Add the cream into a small saucepan. Heat over a medium low heat.

3. When the cream begins to bubble, pour half of the cream into each of the bowls of chocolate. Whisk each bowl until smooth.

4. Cover each bowl with plastic wrap. Chill the bowls for 3 hours.

5. Take the bowls out of the refrigerator. Measure out the filling using a small scoop. Level off the top of the scoop with a knife.

6. Drop the scoops on to a tray lined with parchment paper. Cover the filling loosely with plastic wrap. Chill for at least 1 hour in the refrigerator.

7. Remove the tray from the refrigerator. Take the dropped scoops and roll them into balls between your palms.

8. Divide the balls into two equal groups. Set aside 1/2 to be rolled in toppings.

9. In the other half of the balls insert a toothpick in the center.

10. Insert the other end of the toothpick into a Styrofoam disk or block. Continue this process until all of the balls are on the block.

11. All the rolled balls should be put into the freezer until they are ready to be dipped or coated.

12. The balls without the toothpicks should be rolled in chopped nuts, cocoa powder, or powdered sugar.

13. Next the balls with the toothpicks should be dipped in tempered chocolate, recipe below. Return to the freezer to set.

14. Gently twist the toothpick once the chocolate has set.

15. Seal the toothpick hole with a bit of chocolate.

16. Store the truffles in the refrigerator in an airtight container.

Tempered chocolate:

1. Melt 8 ounces of semi-sweet chocolate in a double boiler with simmering water.

2. Insert a candy thermometer into the chocolate. Remove from heat when the chocolate is 110 degrees F. Dry off the bottom of the bowl. Move the chocolate to another bowl. When the temperature reaches about 90 degrees add the rest of the chocolate. Stir until melted.

CHOCOLATE CHESTNUT TRUFFLES

Makes 12

INGREDIENTS

1 ⅓ cups chestnut flour

⅓ teaspoon sea salt

2 tablespoons unsweetened cocoa powder

½ cup virgin coconut oil

3 tablespoons non-dairy milk

2 teaspoons vanilla extract (optional)

Unsweetened cocoa powder for dusting (optional)

COOKING INSTRUCTIONS

1. Allow for the milk to heat to room temperature or slightly warmer.

2. Gently warm the coconut oil until it is a soft, semi-solid consistency. It should not be quite a liquid, if possible.

3. Mix the chestnut flour, cocoa powder and sea salt in a bowl. Mix in the coconut oil and non-dairy milk. If you are using the vanilla, add it in as well. Mix them well. When done the mixture should have the consistency somewhere between batter and very smooth cookie dough. Put the bowl in the refrigerator for at least 30 to 45 minutes covered in foil or plastic wrap. You can leave it in the refrigerator overnight.

4. After chilling, roll the mixture into small 1-inch balls. Work quickly, it is important not to handle the truffles too long when you are rolling them out. Gently roll the truffle balls into a bit of cocoa powder. For "maximum chestnut" flavor you can roll the truffle in some chestnut flour. Line a baking sheet with parchment or waxed paper. Place the finished truffles on the baking sheet.

5. Chill the truffles in the refrigerator for approximately 20 to 30 minutes.

ABOUT THE AUTHOR

Leslie Taylor was born into a family that loves to cook and loves desserts! His sister is Lisa Joy Taylor, affectionately known as the "Dessert Queen" and the author of *Americas' Most Delicious Dessert Recipes, State by State*. And while his mother was not an author or a professional chef, she was well known throughout her community for exceptional desserts. Not surprisingly both Leslie and Lisa were inspired greatly by their mom and love of good food!

Leslie's background in the culinary arts has been both formal - taking classes and trainings as well as informal - the experience and expertise one can only gain from making thousands upon thousands of desserts! Leslie lives in California with his wife, two daughters and cat Mirabell.

DESSERT RECIPES FOR CHOCOLATE LOVERS!

OTHER BOOKS OF INTEREST
FROM SWEETIE PIE BOOKS!

Available at Amazon.com

www.ingramcontent.com/pod-product-compliance
Lightning Source LLC
Chambersburg PA
CBHW071659090426
42738CB00009B/1587